DIG

DEVELOP IN GRACE

By

Candice Evans

Printed in the United States of America

First Printing, 2025

ISBN: 979-8-9926910-0-9

Publisher: Published by Purpose Publishing House

info@PurposePublishingHouse.com

Dedication

This book is dedicated to my family, friends, and my #1 supporters my mama and my man, my man, my man and our kids, our kids, our kids. I loveth you all. Your belief in me, your grace for me, and your love is represented in the words and stories of this work and for it all I say thank you. With a grateful and humble heart, I thank God for the gift of this work and for trusting me to bring it to life. Your grace has settled me in this season and guided me to bring this book to completion. May this word accomplish all that you intend for those who read it.

Table of Contents

INTRODUCTION

Journey to Develop In Grace (DIG)

Grace is life. It is the gentle whisper of the wind, the soft give of the earth beneath our feet, the sun shining its warmth after the coldest, darkest nights. Grace is the rain, oh, the rain—falling, replenishing, nurturing. Just as the rain waters the earth, so too do our tears water the soil of our lives. Each tear is sacred, a testament to the digging, the searching, and the uncovering of truths that sometimes ache but always nourish. Yes, that's grace.

Grace is not loud; it does not demand attention or accolades. It shows up in the smallest moments—a hand extended in kindness, forgiveness offered when it feels impossible, and the courage to try again when the weight of failure seems too much to bear. Grace meets us where we are, whether we're soaring or scraping rock bottom. It reminds that even in our brokenness, we are whole; even in our mistakes, we are worthy.

Through digging—into the earth, into ourselves—we discover grace in all its quiet power. The act of digging is not without discomfort. It asks us to unearth what we have buried, to sift through the soil of our lives, and to confront the roots we'd rather leave untouched. Yet, in this very act, we invite grace to move. Grace softens the hardened ground of our hearts, making room for growth. Grace gives us the strength to hold what we uncover with tenderness and the courage to let go of what no longer serves us.

My mother, wise as she is, once told me, "There is no life without grace." And oh, how right she is. Grace is woven into every fiber of existence—it is the pulse of the universe, the rhythm of the seasons, the dance of light and shadow. Grace is not something we achieve or deserve; it is the gift of God's love poured out freely, a constant reminder that we are never alone in our journey. What I've learned about grace through digging is this: it doesn't always look like ease.

Sometimes grace shows up in the storm, in the mess, in the breaking. But when the cloud's part, when the soil settles, grace reveals itself in the new life that springs forth. Grace is both the seed and the gardener, the process and the promise. It is what sustains us when we feel we cannot go on, and it is what calls us higher when we are ready to grow.

As I sit here, finishing an introduction to a book I began six years ago, I realize that my journey toward understanding grace began long before I ever gave it a name. Grace, like the roots of a tree, has been a constant companion in my life, shaping me in moments both big and small, even when I wasn't fully aware of it. And just like the roots anchor a tree and draw life from the soil, grace has been that unseen force, grounding me and feeding my growth.

But what does it mean to Develop in Grace—to DIG? Digging is more than just a metaphor for working with soil; it's about going beneath the surface. To DIG is to examine your inner self, unearthing thoughts, feelings, and experiences that shape who you are. It's about confronting the weeds of outdated beliefs or habits and planting seeds of growth and understanding. DIG is also about nurturing relationships and making space for transformation. Just like in a garden, we sometimes have to dig up roots or tend to the soil to help something grow.

Planting Seeds of Grace

One of my earliest encounters with grace came not from what I received but from what I had to dig up inside myself when faced with unexpected challenges, even at a young age.

I was recently talking to my mom about this book and reminiscing about how I've always loved to write. I was first published during my senior year of high school in *Who's Who Among American High School Students* for a poem I wrote called *Struggling to Survive*. But as I reflect, I remember an even earlier moment that truly planted the seeds for my understanding of grace and the journey to DIG. I was in elementary school—the exact grade escapes me. Still, the experience is imprinted on me like the first sprout breaking through the soil. I remember seeing a flier for a school-wide writing contest. I couldn't wait to plant my thoughts on paper, feeling the excitement as my words flowed, and I giggled at my own clever wordplay. Writing was like watering a part of myself that was just beginning to grow, and I was proud of what I had cultivated.

To my joy, I won the contest. I was beyond excited, practically bouncing with happiness, knowing that my writing was not only good but special enough to win. My cheeks hurt from smiling so much, and I couldn't wait to tell my parents and hear them say how proud they were of me. In my young mind, this felt like the best thing that had ever happened.

But my excitement didn't last long. I hadn't realized that winning meant I would have to stand up in front of the entire school and read my poem out loud. The thought made my heart drop straight to my stomach. My chest felt tight, and my hands started to sweat. I couldn't sit still—I was wiggling in my seat, trying to shake off the nervous energy that had suddenly taken over me. My mind raced with thoughts of what might go wrong: What if I messed up? What if everyone laughed? What if I froze and couldn't remember the words?

The idea of standing on that big stage, with all those eyes watching me, felt impossible. I pictured my classmates whispering and pointing, their faces blurry as I tried to focus. It was like I was stuck in one of those bad dreams where you're trying to run, but your legs won't move.

That moment became one of my first encounters with the kind of fear that made my knees feel weak, and my voice shrink to a whisper. It was the beginning of a long struggle with the anxiety of public speaking. But as overwhelming as it was, even that wasn't the hardest part of what was to come.

No, what truly shook me was the experience I had next—a meeting with teachers and administrators. As they called me to the office, I thought it was to discuss the details of sharing my poem at the upcoming assembly. Instead, I was met with suspicion: "We have some questions about your writing," they said. Then, "Where did you get the words from?" and "Did you copy this from a book you read?"

As an avid reader from a young age, I had an expansive vocabulary that often appeared in my writing. But that day, they introduced me to a new word: plagiarism. I was confused at first but soon realized what was happening—they were accusing me of something I didn't even fully understand.

I felt shaky, alone, hurt, and angry. I wanted to cry, but even then, it was as though my mother's voice was already there, whispering what she would later tell me as an adult when I shared another experience rooted in prejudice: **'Don't let them see you cry.'** But even as a little girl, I had something inside me, a strength, a grace that I didn't yet fully understand. Like a tree's roots digging deeper into the soil to find nourishment in harsh conditions, I found the grace I needed to stand my ground. My emotions were raw and on display, but my voice, although shaky, did not falter. I explained, advocated for myself, and watched as their accusations softened. It took far too much effort for them to believe me, to see me. But I stood my ground, and eventually, they backed off.

A few days later, I stood at that podium in front of my peers, in front of those who had doubted me, and I read my winning poem aloud. That was grace in action, sprouting through the rocky soil of doubt and adversity. Even at that tender age, I had begun to dig—into myself, into my strength, into the grace that would carry me through.

I didn't hold that experience against my teacher. I didn't stop writing. And I haven't stopped. However, as I sit here now, I wonder if that experience planted a seed of imposter syndrome that lingered for far too long. I have poem after poem, book after book, that, for many years, stayed on paper or were lost in forgotten files. But now, I'm digging up those words again, finding them in the cloud, finding grace, and sharing my writing. Sharing *my* story of *DIG*.

That experience planted something in me—both a wound and a lesson. Although I didn't stop writing, and I didn't stop using my voice, my voice was not as loud, and my writing was tinged with questioning and hesitation. I carried that doubt with me, unsure whether my words would be met with recognition or resistance. But still, I wrote. I didn't fully realize then how much that moment shaped me, how much it made me question where I belonged, how much of myself I needed to unearth.

And that's what *Develop in Grace* is about. Grace is a gift freely given, yes. But just like a gardener must tend to their plants, how we operate in grace—how we nurture and display it to ourselves and others—is something that requires intentionality and care. This is an invitation—not just to read, but to DIG. To unearth, to question, to soften, and to grow. Grace has been here all along, waiting beneath the surface. Now, it's time to cultivate it. It's time to DIG.

CHAPTER 1

Rooted in Grace

"The deeper the roots, the stronger the tree."
– African Proverb

Grace has always been a quiet companion in my life, guiding me before I even knew its name. From a young age, I felt its presence—a whisper calling me to something deeper. I was often the "listening friend," the one people trusted with their stories, sensing I would hold them with care. Even before I could articulate it, grace was already working, already rooting itself within me. There was a curiosity in me about people—their struggles, their joy, their pain—and an almost unspoken invitation to hold space for them.

Seeds of Grace

"Grace is the soil from which we grow, nurturing our roots even when the ground feels hard."

When I reached high school, that invitation deepened when I shadowed a social worker. I remember accompanying her on home visits, stepping into the lives of families at difficult crossroads. I watched as she engaged with people experiencing unimaginable struggles, each carrying burdens they may have hidden from even their closest friends or family. Children who repeatedly came to school with lice in

17

their hair and complaints of hunger, parents weighed down by stress or lack of resources, teens dealing with addiction issues— each encounter offered me a glimpse into the rawness of life's hardships. Witnessing these moments stirred something in me: a sense of empathy, responsibility, and an understanding of grace I hadn't yet named. I felt a sense of being guided somewhere meaningful. **In those moments, I saw how grace wasn't just a concept—it was a necessity, a lifeline extended in times of need.**

Little did I know that seeds of grace were being planted in me through those experiences—seeds that would keep me rooted through life's toughest seasons, not just for myself, but to hold space and extend grace to others. Grace isn't something I sought—it found me. In the still moments of my life, when I felt unseen and unheard, grace was there, quietly wrapping itself around my soul, urging me to breathe, to release, to be. Much like a seed nestled in the soil, unseen and quiet but full of potential, grace was there, nurturing me beneath the surface. It prepared me to break through the hard ground of life's challenges, reaching for the light and finding the strength to grow. Just as the soil anchors and feeds the roots of a plant, grace has been the quiet force grounding me, unseen but always present.

Words as Seeds

Recently, at a family gathering, I was talking with my cousin about relationships, financial setbacks, and the challenges of adulting in today's world. We were sharing the weight of our struggles, and I said, "Sometimes when things aren't going right, you just have to go to sleep." He stopped mid-sentence and said, "That's a word right there." In our conversation, "that's a word" meant more than just agreement—it meant "that's a seed."

Words, like seeds, have the power to grow, take root, and produce something meaningful in our lives. Growing up, going to sleep was a seed of grace, a small act of surrender that allowed me to let go, rest, and be renewed. It was a reminder that grace doesn't always come in grand gestures; sometimes, it's found in the simplest acts of self-care and trust.

One day, I saw this same wisdom in my daughter during one of our walks and talks. Out of the blue, she said, "If Ronnie—let's call him that—rejects me, I'm going to cry, listen to sad music, and then go to sleep and not think about him anymore." I stopped and looked at her, smiling. "Well, isn't that wise?" I thought to myself. At that moment, I remember thinking, *She's going to be okay.* Even at her age, she was intuitively giving herself grace—acknowledging her feelings, letting herself feel them, and then letting them go. She was choosing stillness, rest, and renewal, just as I've always believed in saying, "Go to sleep." It amazed me how naturally she made that connection. She was finding her own sense of grace in her own way. These moments, whether in my own life or in my daughter's, remind me that grace isn't something we have to work hard to find—it's something we allow ourselves to experience. Sometimes, it's as simple as giving yourself permission to rest, trusting that renewal will come like a plant, trusting the soil to nourish its roots as it grows toward the light.

I like to think that grace is the soil from which we grow, nurturing our roots even when the ground feels hard. It is the quiet force that supports our growth, often unseen but always present. These lessons of grace—its quiet presence, its nurturing force—were not confined to my personal life. They became the foundation I would carry into my professional journey. As my career unfolded, I found myself holding space for people in unimaginable ways—as a therapist, a social worker, and, especially, in hospice with those nearing the end of life. In this role, I heard stories that could knock you over with their weight. I accompanied people at their lowest points, hearing their deepest, most vulnerable truths—sometimes

"Grace is the quiet force that reminds us to seek connection, to offer forgiveness, and to embrace growth."

truths they hadn't even shared with their closest friends or loved ones. I sat with people who were counting down not years but hours or even minutes. In those moments, it was vital to stay rooted upright and anchored in grace.

21

Grace Anchoring

Grace allowed me to listen without judgment, to keep my heart open without falling apart. I had to trust that my roots would keep me steady, allowing me to be soft, even in seasons that felt impossibly hard. In those spaces, grace became both my strength and my softness, my way of bearing witness without breaking, of being present without becoming overwhelmed. This grounding has been, and will always be, the foundation of my work, calling, and life's journey. I learned that true strength isn't found in what we can endure alone but in the grace we give ourselves to be vulnerable, to lean on others, and to soften into who we are meant to become.

The tears that flowed from my childhood pain were like seeds, taking root and grounding me in grace. Over time, those seeds of grace have borne fruit, spreading wide and far. My family is where these seeds were first planted. We're a tight-knit group, and while we've had our share of conflicts—hurtful words, missed opportunities, times when we didn't show up for each other—the seeds of grace that were planted long ago have created a foundation that has held us together. Like the deep roots of a tree, our family ties are the lifeblood that nourishes us through every season, keeping us grounded in love and history.

Through the story of Jesus in the Bible, I found a deeper understanding of grace—one that transcends boundaries and speaks to the core of humanity. His life demonstrated that true strength comes not from power or control but from humility, forgiveness, and love. Grace, as reflected in his actions, has the power to heal, to restore, and to transform. These lessons have been a profound source of guidance, shaping how I navigate relationships, challenges, and even my own sense of self. While my understanding of grace has been deeply influenced by the Bible, I believe its essence is universal. Grace is the quiet force that reminds us to seek connection, offer forgiveness, and embrace growth. Whether we find it in sacred teachings, personal reflections, or life's smallest moments, grace invites us all to soften, surrender, and rise stronger.

For me, grace is not merely a concept or an idea; it is a lived experience, a spiritual path that has shaped my life in profound ways. My journey with grace deepened as I entered adulthood, especially when I became a mother. Motherhood was a revelation—a beautiful, messy, exhausting journey that demanded more of me than I ever thought I could give. There were days when I felt utterly overwhelmed and moments when I thought I was failing. But every time I reached my breaking point, grace was there, reminding me that I didn't have to do it all perfectly and I was enough just as I was.

This book is my offering to you—a testament to the power of grace. It's an invitation to walk with me on this path, to explore the depths of your own soul, to dig deep and discover the grace that lies within you. Together, we will uncover the hidden roots, the stories that shape us, the experiences that define us, and through it all, we will find the strength to grow, thrive, and become.

Grace is not something that happens to us; it's something we cultivate, something we become. Much like the soil that nourishes a plant, our soul is where grace takes root and grows. Just as the soil must be tended, enriched, and sometimes broken to allow seeds to flourish, our souls must be nurtured with care, love, and patience. In the same way that the soil anchors the roots of a tree, grace anchors our growth, helping us rise even in the hardest seasons.

Grace is the force that has shaped my life, the light that has guided me through my darkest moments, and the hand that has held me up when I thought I couldn't stand. And as we journey together, remember that grace is not a destination—it's the journey itself, the unfolding

"Growth isn't always found on the surface, it's often buried deep within the soil..."

of our true selves, the deepening of our roots. As you read, may you find the courage to unearth what's been buried, to tend to what's growing, and to trust in the grace that has been with you all along.

In writing this book, I had to Develop in Grace (DIG) and, as you read each chapter, I invite you to DIG too:

 **In writing this book, I had to Develop in Grace (DIG) and, as you read each chapter, I invite you to DIG too:**

1. How does the concept of grace as both softness and strength resonate with your experiences?

_____

_____

_____

2. How can you apply this understanding of grace to your current relationships or challenges?

_____

_____

_____

3. Where in your life could you allow more grace? How might accepting grace from others change the way you navigate your challenges?

_____

_____

_____

Continue to DIG

_____

_____

_____

_____

_____

_____

_____

_____

_____

_____

_____

_____

_____

Rooted Blessing

Before a seed ever breaks through the soil, it must surrender to the dark. It softens, cracks open, and trusts that what it needs will find its way to it. It does not resist growth—it yields to it.

May you be open to developing in grace. May you trust that even in unseen places, transformation is happening. May you lean into the process, knowing that stretching, reaching, and deepening are all part of becoming. You do not have to force growth—grace is already doing the work beneath the surface.

-DIG

CHAPTER 2

Facing the Dragon: Unearthing Past Traumas

"You don't have to dig deep to find the wounds; the real work is in finding the grace between."

– Maya Angelou

Real growth begins beneath the surface. To truly thrive, we must DIG—into the roots of our past, into the places we've buried pain, and into the tangled depths of our experiences. The work of unearthing isn't always easy, but it's necessary. Growth doesn't just happen—it requires excavation, courage, and grace. The same can be said for grace as it relates to our soul. But only you can decide when to go beneath the surface to confront what's been buried—the pain, the traumas, and the stories that shape who you are. For many years, I resisted this process. I believed I could live above ground, bypass the pain, and skip the digging, thinking I'd be fine as long as I kept moving. But the truth is, real growth only came when I began the small act of digging deep and embraced the bigger journey of DIG—Developing in Grace.

One of the most challenging parts of this journey was acknowledging my own internal "Dragon," a powerful force wrapped up within my root system. My Dragon is a part of me I've come to know well—though for years, I pretended it didn't exist. It's a force that rears up with anger, defensiveness, and a fierce desire to protect. For a long time, I carried it in silence, mistaking its presence for my identity. I thought my Dragon defined me—that its fire was the only thing keeping me strong. But the truth is, while I believed I bore it alone, my Dragon was anything but silent. Its fire spoke in my reactions, in my defenses, in the moments when I felt the need to shield myself from pain. I wasn't just carrying it—I was feeding it. When it erupted, it was raw and vivid, impossible for those close to me to ignore. What I felt as an internal storm was experienced by others in living color—fierce, intense, and unmistakably real. The Dragon's roar wasn't confined to my inner world; it spilled out, impacting those around me in ways I hadn't fully realized.

The Dragon grew strong and tangled in the depths of my soil, feeding on old wounds, the relentless patterns of survival mode, and the reactive instincts passed down through my roots. Growing up, I absorbed the generational patterns sent from my family's legacy—messages of resilience, strength, and fire. Survival mode wasn't just something I experienced; it was woven into the soil I came from. Operating in this way— sometimes silently, sometimes erupting—shaped my responses to the world around me. The fire of my Dragon wasn't just a personal force; it carried the echoes of a history of needing to be strong, of reacting in ways that protected but didn't always nurture. That history shaped me, but it didn't define all of me.

Understanding Violence and Grace

Recently, I was talking with my brother about anger, and we agreed that it often gets a bad rap. People who display anger are often misunderstood, labeled as having a "problem," and pushed toward managing or suppressing it. He reminded me that anger itself isn't the problem—it's what we do with it.

I reflected on how, in an argument or even when wanting to get my point across, I sometimes cry, or my voice shakes. The intensity of my feelings overwhelms me, leaving me struggling to verbally articulate and advocate my thoughts. In those moments, I judge myself harshly. I see my tears and trembling voice as a sign of weakness, as though I'm not in control of myself. It's a discomfort that comes from within- a frustration with my own vulnerability. One example of this is how I introduced a group of friends to Spicy Uno, a game they now love but one I dread playing with them at times. When things get "spicy" in Uno, everyone starts arguing, debating, and litigating their points; my body reacts in the present day like it's reliving the past. It's a powerful reminder of how deeply our past can linger. As *The Body Keeps the Score* explains, our bodies hold onto what we've experienced, sometimes more vividly than our minds.

It's not that I can't keep up, but I feel my Dragon stirring in those moments. While my friends seem comfortable expressing their frustrations through words, I never quite learned to process anger that way. I come from a family where even Spades and a game of Go Fish could erupt into "I Declare War!". Calm and patient conversations were not the norm in those instances—there might be slamming the table, storming off, or a heated exchange instead.

As I have done the work of digging into my roots, I began to confront the ways violence had shown up in my life—not just outwardly, in heated exchanges, but inwardly as well. I realized that the patterns of outward intensity often mirrored the inner struggles I carried. This reflection brought new clarity, especially as I read Deborah Adele's teachings in *The Yamas & Niyamas*. In her chapter on ahimsa, or nonviolence, she describes how violence is not limited to physical acts or acts with others. Violence can look like speaking unkind words, being harsh with ourselves, or feeling hurried, afraid, and out of balance. This struck a chord with me because I realized how often I had been violent toward myself. My rigid expectations, my harsh self-talk, and the fear that kept me in reactive cycles were forms of internal violence that I had normalized.

Adele's teachings also helped me see how living out of balance fosters violence against ourselves and others. When we live in survival mode, trapped in the cycles of stress and cortisol, we lose our ability to respond with compassion. I saw how my Dragon thrived in this imbalance. Its fire wasn't inherently bad, but when left unchecked, it burned in ways that harmed me and those I loved. Adele's emphasis on cultivating self-love as a foundation for nonviolence resonated deeply. She writes that how we treat ourselves sets the tone for how we treat others.

Grace became my tool for practicing Ahimsa—not perfection, but progress.

There was a time when I believed that the Dragon's fire was all there was to me. But through grace and the teachings of Ahimsa, I began to see the possibility of living differently. My fire didn't have to be destructive; it could be a source of warmth, illumination, and transformation. Adele's words

"When we listen to our anger-to understand what it's trying to protect or advocate for-it becomes a tool for growth."

reminded me that violence often masks itself in worry, fear, or control—things I had mistaken for care or strength. Learning to step out of those cycles and loosen the Dragon's grip was an act of grace in itself.

Reframing the Dragon and Its Fire

Fire has always been a symbol of transformation—it can destroy, but it can also warm, illuminate, and inspire. Anger, much like fire, often gets a bad reputation. It's viewed as a problem to solve, a beast to tame, or a fault to correct. But what if anger isn't the problem? What if it's the misuse, misunderstanding, or repression of anger that causes harm?

For years, the Dragon's fire felt like something to be feared. It manifested in loud outbursts, impatience, and rigid ways of thinking. Other times, it showed up as silence—holding everything in to avoid the risk of my fire scorching those around me. It wasn't just about anger; it was about being so activated that I didn't trust myself to respond gently. My hands would tremble, my body ached with the tension of holding everything inside, and I felt disconnected from my sense of self. Even today, that trembling remains—a physical manifestation of the energy within me, a reminder of how deeply the fire runs.

For a long time, I saw that trembling as something to hide, something that would make people question me. I worried they might think I was weak, unstable, or even unwell. People have asked me if I'm okay, if I'm coming off of something, or if I'm ill. The questions cut deep, reinforcing my shame and fear of the fire within me. But one day, everything shifted when a pastor at a church training prophesied over me. She told me my trembling wasn't a weakness or a flaw—it was the mark of an activator.

Her words aligned with what I was learning through Internal Family Systems (IFS), a therapeutic approach developed by Dr. Richard C. Schwartz that taught me to see my mind as an internal landscape with different "parts." In IFS, we named our parts, and I came to know this fiery part of me as the Dragon. Through IFS, I learned that the Dragon was not my enemy—it was a protector. The pastor's prophecy further solidified this understanding. She reframed what I had always seen as a negative, helping me understand that my fire wasn't meant to harm but to ignite. This revelation helped me see how my fire could inspire, uplift, and activate others in meaningful ways. It wasn't something to fear or suppress; it was something to embrace and guide with care (Schwartz, 1995).

Through my work as a youth leader, I began to see how this activation could bring life to others. Whether leading children's church or facilitating grief groups in schools, I poured out my energy to ignite hope and connection. My fire helped children find laughter in difficult moments, share their stories, and build community. What I once feared as destructive became a tool for light and growth. Anger is a signal. It speaks to our values, our boundaries, and the things we hold dear. It reveals our unmet needs, our sense of injustice, or the places we've been hurt. When we deny anger or suppress it, we often miss the deeper message it carries. But when we learn to listen to our anger—to understand what it's trying to protect or advocate for—it becomes a tool for growth.

Digging with Grace

The work in IFS isn't about removing parts of ourselves but about harmonizing them, creating space for each to breathe. My Dragon had been on guard, entangled deep within my root system, always ready to defend. But as I began to unearth these roots, I learned that I am more than just my Dragon; I am also the one who can calm it, the one who can gently disentangle it from the old stories and hardened soil of survival.

Digging into this work has required me to unlearn many beliefs I held about strength and resilience. I used to think that if something was hard, it meant it was good, and pushing through pain was a sign of strength. But I've come to understand that everything hard isn't good. Living with tangled roots doesn't mean I'm thriving—it means I'm surviving in survival mode. Now, I am learning to find strength in softness, to thrive in ease and peace, and to recognize that true resilience allows for rest and tenderness.

As I continued to untangle the Dragon from my roots, I began to notice how it influenced my relationships. For years, I carried a shield—a tension that kept others at a distance. Yet there were those who saw beyond the shield, who sensed the light inside the belly of the Dragon, the warmth beneath the intensity. They found me fun, exciting, and even vibrant. It was a delicate balance—being guarded, inviting, intense, and warm. Grace has shown me that the true power of the Dragon lies not in its defense but in its ability to rest, to allow for connection, and to release itself from old tangles.

The Flip Side of the Dragon

As I've learned to navigate my Dragon, I've also come to appreciate its flip side. As I've learned to navigate my Dragon, I've come to understand that its fire was never the enemy—it was how I used it that mattered. When I stopped fearing the flames, I saw that fire wasn't just destruction; it was warmth, passion, creativity, and even joy. The flip side of my Dragon wasn't about suppression—it was about transformation. In my friend group, I bring what I like to call the "fun factor." I ignite energy and laughter, creating an atmosphere where people never know what they're going to get from me. Whether it's a witty remark or an unexpected idea, my fire activates joy and connection in those moments.

In my family, this fire has taken on a more intentional role. I bring a different way of seeing things, encouraging us to try new approaches while staying rooted in traditions that serve us well. I've embraced a more natural, herbal way of living, incorporating remedies and practices that may seem unconventional at first but often open doors to healing and connection. My willingness to try "weird" things—whether it's eating something unfamiliar or using natural methods for wellness—sparks curiosity and creates space for exploration and growth within my family.

In my extended family, I bring stories back to life. Whether it's retelling memories that make us laugh or reinterpreting moments with a fresh perspective, I use my energy to preserve our history while keeping it alive and relevant for today. My fire is both grounding and inspiring, helping us remember where we came from while considering where we want to go.

In my professional life, I'm often called an activator of ideas, a visionary who sparks creativity and ignites others to think differently. I'm frequently consulted for strategic planning, brainstorming, and co-creating solutions. My colleagues have referred to me as an "idea fountain," a phrase that makes me smile because it reflects how my fire, when directed, inspires others to take action and bring new ideas to life.

One of the most meaningful activities I developed when I worked for a hospice organization as a School-Based Grief

Counselor was *The Flip Side of Grief.* Just as I strive not to get stuck in the overwhelming side of my dragon, I don't want grieving youth to remain stuck in the pain of their loss. So, I designed an activity to help them process their grief and move toward hope and healing. The activity began with a simple sheet of paper divided into two sides. On one side, they explored the "who, what, when, where, and why" of their grief—the story of their loss. They wrote about the day everything changed, the emotions they felt, and the lingering sense of absence in their lives.

Then, we turned to the flip side. On this side, they shifted their focus to the present and future—the "who, what, when, where, and why" of their lives now. This was where grace entered the picture. Many teens began sharing what they were looking forward to: a school dance, earning their driver's license, or a college acceptance letter. They talked about their dreams and the people encouraging them along the way.

This activity showed them—and reminded me—that grief doesn't have to be the final word in their story. There is always a flip side, a place where grace meets us and helps us move forward. It was inspiring to witness these young people shift from being overwhelmed by their past to embracing the possibilities of their future.

When I reflect on my life, I realize that I've always sought to ignite that same hope, whether as a social worker, a youth leader, or simply in my relationships. The flip side of my Dragon isn't about denying its fire—it's about using that fire to warm, illuminate, and inspire. It's about igniting possibility in myself and others, turning pain into purpose, and creating something meaningful out of what might otherwise feel like ashes.

Family, Dragons, and Community

My family and I have begun naming and facing our Dragons together. I've shared my journey with them, encouraging them to explore the parts of themselves that rise up in moments of stress or fear. For me, it's the Dragon. For others, it might be something entirely different. One of my friends named her part the Octopus, always grabbing at too many things and saying yes when she needed to say no. These conversations have been challenging but deeply healing, allowing us to support one another in untangling our roots and embracing grace.

Grace has given me the strength to let down the shield, to trust that my fire can light the way without scorching those around me. And as we all face our Dragons, we are learning that the process of digging deep and untangling our roots is where the real growth happens. I've learned that when I feel the Dragon waking, I don't need to suppress it or explode. Instead, I've found healthier ways to release that fire. I can dance it out. I can walk it out. I can write it out. Sometimes, I simply move away from the situation or person until I'm ready to speak. And when I do open my mouth, I trust that my voice—not my fire—will come out.

It's not about perfection; it's about progress, about finding the courage to dig, release, and grow in grace.

 ## We and all of our parts deserve to DIG:

1. I call mine the Dragon. What do you call yours, and how does it show up in your life?

_____

_____

_____

2. What old beliefs or patterns might be keeping your roots tangled?

_____

_____

_____

3. How can you begin to untangle your roots with grace?

_____

_____

_____

4. Who do you feel safe enough to let in past your shield?

_____

_____

_____

5. How has anger impacted positive change or advocacy for self or others?

_____

_____

_____

Continue to DIG

_____

_____

_____

_____

_____

_____

_____

_____

_____

_____

_____

_____

_____

_____

Grace-Filled Tears

I operated in a sphere that if you upset me enough to bring a tear to my eye, before the tear could fall, start the match the fight was on.

The layers of pain, hurt, and mistrust behind this belief took years and many fallen tears to uncover.

Now I know my tears are my strength, each drop falls to the earth, giving life to the roots that hold me up. I cry because I care; I care about you; no violence will heal your pain.

I care about me and have found that for me, it is the same. The pain remains if the tears don't fall. The pain returns, laying claim to victory over my soul, no sense of control over me, my pain, my life, over mine. It's mine for the taking, check your word, it is so.

Yet, authority escapes the wounded; grab it quick and don't let go. The worthy wear the crown, not mask, no masquerade, welcome to your ball.

Show up for yourself; there's grace when the tears fall.

The grace in me honors the grace in you—DIG

CHAPTER 3

Cultivating Stillness

"Be still, and know that I am God."

– (Psalm 46:10 New International Version)

In a world that glorifies noise and constant movement, stillness can feel elusive, even unnatural. Yet stillness is where I find my deepest peace, clearest thoughts, and the grace that sustains me through life's uncertainties. Stillness isn't simply the absence of movement; it's an intentional presence of mind, a decision to pause—not just to recharge, but to remember who I am beneath the layers of life's demands.

For years, I thought self-care was something outside of myself—a luxury reserved for the spa, a manicure, or a vacation I often couldn't afford. In my mind, self-care remained a distant privilege, something to be earned. But slowly, I came to see stillness as a way to truly nourish my soul, a form of self-care that required no money, no elaborate plan, and no escape from my daily life. It needed only me and the decision to pause.

Stillness, I've learned, is much like digging into the soil. It's about breaking through the surface, creating space for something new to grow. Stillness is the act of sinking into the soil, trusting that, even when unseen, grace is nurturing your roots. Just as the plant rests in the soil during dormant seasons, stillness allows us to rest in God's sufficiency, knowing His power is at work even in our quiet, vulnerable moments. Digging doesn't always look pretty or feel productive in the moment, but it is essential. Just as a gardener prepares the ground before planting, I've found that stillness prepares me for life's seasons of growth. In stillness, I dig inward, tending to the parts of myself that often go unnoticed. I reflect on my thoughts, my emotions, and my heart—not to fix them, but to understand and nurture them.

"Stillness is the act of sinking into the soil, trusting that, even when unseen, grace is nurturing your roots."

It's in these quiet moments that I create space for grace to take root, for the unseen work of growth to begin.

Everyday Moments of Stillness

Stillness doesn't always come naturally. There are days when distractions tempt me when I find myself mindlessly scrolling or, as my Papa would often say, "making tracks but not getting anywhere." Yet I've learned that stillness doesn't have to be grand or perfect—it can be found in the simplest of moments.

Growing up, I was a fast eater, rushing through meals without tasting them. Before I knew it, I'd finished, often unsatisfied, reaching for something sweet to fill what I'd missed. Later, I learned about mindful eating—a way to engage with food slowly, with purpose. I remember practicing with a single piece of chocolate, holding it, feeling its shape and weight, smelling it, and, finally, letting it melt slowly in my mouth. I noticed textures, flavors, and sensations I'd overlooked in my haste.

At that moment, I realized I'd been living my life much like I'd been eating—fast, distracted, and always looking for the next thing to satisfy me. Just as I learned to slow down with that small piece of chocolate, I've had to learn to pace my life with grace.

Stillness also comes in moments of connection with my children. Watching them play at the park or laugh with each other, I've learned to pause and simply be present. In their joy, I've found a reminder to savor what's here right now. Stillness, in these moments, becomes a gift of connection—not just with them, but with myself.

Prayer as a Form of Tending

One of the most profound ways I cultivate stillness is through prayer. I once thought of prayer as simply asking for things, but over time, it became a sanctuary of peace. In prayer, I quiet my mind, open my heart, and let the words come, if they come at all. Sometimes, prayer is just silence—the feeling of being held by something greater than myself.

Prayer has become a way of tending to my spirit, much like watering a garden. It roots me in what's important, slowing me down and aligning me with grace. In prayer, I find a peace that surpasses understanding, a grace that says I am enough, even without doing anything more. It has become a time to pause and allow myself to be without rushing to do or to fix. Stillness, I've learned, is about creating space—not just for rest but for growth. It's about tending to the soil of your life, breaking through the hard ground of busyness and distraction to nurture what lies beneath. Just as a gardener knows that the most important work happens underground, I've come to see that stillness is where the deepest transformation takes place.

When I look beyond the impact of stillness in my life, I find inspiration in cultures that embrace slower, simpler ways of living. In many Eastern traditions, practices like meditation, tai chi, and yoga cultivate inner stillness, a quiet focus that extends into each day. Similarly, Scandinavian cultures have *hygge*—a word that means finding coziness and comfort in simple pleasures. Whether it's sharing tea with a friend or walking in silence, it's a way of savoring life as it is.

I also think of Indigenous cultures, which have long emphasized the importance of harmony with the earth and the power of sitting still with nature. Many Indigenous teachings encourage listening—not just to others but to the land, the wind, and the rhythms of the natural world. This quiet communion with nature is a form of stillness that reconnects us to something greater, reminding us that we are part of a larger cycle of life. These cultures teach that in stillness, we honor both the earth and ourselves, finding wisdom in the pauses and peace in simply being.

Together, these cultures remind me that stillness doesn't have to be something we "do." It's something we allow ourselves to experience—a moment of grace that simply invites us to be.

The Courage to Be Still

In the Western world, we often equate busyness with success, fearing that slowing down will leave us behind. But stillness isn't about being left behind; it's about moving forward with intention. It's a conscious choice to pause, to reflect, and to gather strength for what lies ahead.

Even now, I have days when I'm tempted to distract myself, to fill every moment with something to do. But I think back to a game we played as children—the *Quiet Game*, where we'd see who could stay silent the longest. Back then, it was just a fun challenge, a playful way to pass the time. But as an adult, I see its wisdom. Stillness, I now know, is an act of courage. It's not about winning or enduring silence for its own sake but about finding the strength to be with myself and to let grace meet me there.

"Stillness, I've learned, is not about escaping life but about finding peace within it."

Stillness, I've learned, is not about escaping life but about finding peace within it. Just as my grandmother knew that the breeze would come when we paused, I've learned to trust that peace will find me when I make room for it. I don't have to run from the noise, the responsibilities, or even the struggles. I only need to be still and let grace meet me, just as I am.'

 ## Be still and know that you can DIG:

1. Reflect on what it feels like to be still, even if only for a moment, and notice what comes up when you make space for grace.

_____

_____

_____

2. Consider the areas of life where you might be rushing through, and explore what it would look like to pause and truly savor those moments.

_____

_____

_____

3. Allow yourself to embrace the quiet seasons, like winter, trusting that in stillness, deep inner work is taking place.

_____

_____

_____

4. Take inspiration from cultures that value stillness and simplicity. How can you bring more of that peace and intentionality into your own life?

_____

_____

_____

Continue to DIG

_____

_____

_____

_____

_____

_____

_____

_____

_____

_____

_____

_____

_____

_____

_____

INTERLUDE

Be. Still. Know.

I invite you to sit or lie comfortably. Begin taking intentional breaths as you quiet your mind. With each inhale and exhale, notice that you have become more relaxed. As thoughts come, allow them to go. Continue to fill your belly with air as you inhale and release the air from your belly with your exhale. Continue breathing until you are ready, and repeat the following phrases to yourself. Be still and know that...

I am rooted and supported.

I am worthy of every breath, every moment, and every blessing.

I am a reflection of resilience.

I am the soil, the seed, the harvest, and the rest.

Thank you for pausing to be still and know.

Taking this moment to reflect is a gift you've given yourself, a step toward cultivating grace in your life. I encourage you to create some affirmations of your ow, allowing your words to reflect the grace you are growing into. If these affirmations have resonated with you, I invite you to explore the appendix at the back of this book, where you'll find a full collection of affirmations to support your journey, where you'll find a full collection to support your journey. Remember you never journey in grace alone. Part of living a grace-filled life is not just about how we extend grace towards self, but how we offer it to those we are connected to.

CHAPTER 4

The Beauty of Connectedness

"We are all connected, just like the branches of a tree are connected to the trunk."

– Candice Evans

Growing up in a military family, my life was one of constant uprooting. Just like a plant moved from pot to pot, I adapted to new soil with each place we landed—Georgia, Germany, Kentucky, Tennessee, Alaska, Iowa, and finally back to the birth state of my parents, Missouri. Each new start became another chapter in my journey. I learned to make friends quickly, connect with new surroundings, and settle into routines, all the while knowing these roots wouldn't run deep. With each move, I learned to guard my heart, keeping something back to make the goodbyes easier. My life was a rhythm of planting, growing, uprooting, and moving on.

Through all the transitions, my family remained my grounding force. They were my true roots. Like the deep roots of a tree, our family ties became my lifeblood, sustaining me through every season, even when everything else felt temporary. We weren't tied to any one place; we were tied to each other. The values, stories, and shared love we carried gave me a sense of home, even in the most unsettling moments.

Grace in the Family

If you were to ask me who has taught me the most about grace, I wouldn't hesitate to say, "my family." They are my biggest grace teachers, hands down. And let me tell you—the family will test every ounce of grace you have. You know the saying, "The people closest to you hurt you the most"? That's because they know you best. When Michelle Obama says, "When they go low, we go high," I think, *Yeah, but when your family goes low, they go reeeeal low. They know exactly where to aim.*

As someone whose love language is words of affirmation, what people say to me—or about me—carries weight. A thoughtless comment from family can sting deeper than I care to admit. Growing up, there were times when things were said that left me angry, hurt, and ready to retreat into my own world. And yet, grace always found its way back into those relationships. Whether it came through an apology, a shared laugh, or simply the passage of time softening the edges, grace was always at work, like the unseen hands of a skilled potter reshaping what felt broken.

Looking back, I think of our household as a "House of Grace." Not because we always got it right—far from it—but because we always found a way to repair it. Grace has been the quiet glue holding us together when tempers flared, misunderstandings festered, or words cut too deep.

Even now, in the family I've built with my husband and children, grace is the undercurrent. There are days when I'm searching for grace like it's a set of keys. *Is it in the kitchen cabinet? The shower? Maybe in the fridge next to the milk?* Because let's be real, my husband gets on my last nerve sometimes, and I know I do the same for him. Yet grace shows up, nudging us back to each other. It whispers, *Take a breath. You're both doing your best.*

"Without roots, there is no foundation to thrive, no connection to sustain us."

Grace has taught me that the family unit—whether it's the one you're born into or the one you create—is sustained not by perfection but by forgiveness, patience, and repair. I've met people who are estranged from their families, and while I respect their journeys, it always sits heavy on my heart. For me, grace is the bridge that keeps those ties from breaking entirely.

Of course, it's not always easy. There have been moments of "block and delete" on social media, heated arguments, and even the occasional dramatic phone hang-up. But grace invites us to come back, to have the hard conversations, to soften the anger, and to rebuild what's been strained. It's a practice, a muscle we have to keep strengthening.

Rooted in Family

My parents come from big families, and they instilled in us the importance of connection and responsibility. They didn't always emphasize emotional well-being as gentle or conscious parents of today might, but they taught us practical grace in action: family was everything. We were expected to show up for one another, to apologize when we were wrong, and to repair what was broken.

Even now, when my family gathers from different parts of the country or just around St. Louis, it's as though no time has passed. We fall right back into sync, picking up where we left off. It's not just a connection; it's a remembering. We remember we are family. We remember our roots. That sense of grounding is what gives me strength and resilience. This deep connection has shaped the way I see myself and the world around me. When you see me, you're seeing the reflection of those roots—the resilience and connection that have carried me through the circumstances of life, even as my path has diverged from my family's.

The beauty of roots is that they stay with you no matter where you are. Roots signal life and the potential for growth, reminding us that without roots, there is no foundation to thrive, no connection to sustain us. One of the most fascinating truths I've learned about plants and trees is their connection to the soil from which they first grew. Studies like those shared in *The Hidden Life of Trees* by Peter Wohlleben reveal how roots retain a memory of their original environment, even when transplanted to new locations. Similarly, plants carry genetic and environmental imprints that shape their growth, regardless of where they are replanted.

This concept resonates deeply with me. While I've moved from place to place, my connection to my family and the values they instilled in me has never faded. It's as if the "soil" of my childhood remains with me, nourishing me wherever I go. No matter how far I've traveled or how much I've grown, those original roots are still a part of me. They remind me that home isn't always a physical place—it's a connection to the people and principles that ground us.

Lessons for the Next Generation

I try to pass this legacy of connection on to my own children. When they fight or test each other's patience—as siblings often do—I remind them that one day, they will need each other. When my son teases his sister endlessly, pushing her limits, I am quick to tell him, "There will come a time when you'll need her, and no one else will be there like your family."

This belief in the enduring strength of family doesn't mean every relationship is perfect. I know some people are estranged from their families, and for valid reasons. I've seen how some connections can become toxic or poisonous, draining the very life they should be nurturing. Grace, for me, has meant learning when to hold on and when to let go. Some relationships need to be severed or pruned in order for someone to restore their health and thrive. If that's your story, I encourage you to build healthy connections of your own. The beauty of connection is that it doesn't have to look one specific way.

For me, my connections are deeply rooted in family. They're not perfect, but they are my foundation. One of my favorite quotes, "To thine own self be true," resonates because I believe the greatest connection we can nurture is the one with ourselves. The more you DIG into who you are, the more beautiful your connections will be—wherever and with whomever they form. Grace has taught me that. The strength of these family ties became even more evident during one of the most challenging transitions of my life.

When I was 16 years old, my father received a compassionate reassignment after learning that his father—my grandfather—was dying. Within 24 hours, we packed up our lives in Germany and were on a plane back to the States. The speed of it all left no room for goodbyes or reflection. I remember the rush of packing, the tears we didn't have time to cry, and the overwhelming sense of displacement as we left behind not just a home but the relationships and routines I had begun to build.

That move was anything but a sweet 16. At an age where I was beginning to discover who I was, I felt the weight of leaving yet

"Friendships are steady roots that remind me of where I've been, ground me in who I am, and keep me looking forward to memories we've yet to make "The deepest connections are those rooted in grace."

another chapter behind, this time under the shadow of loss and grief. The abruptness of it all required me to dig into a resilience I didn't even know I had. Like certain plants that conserve energy when uprooted, I learned to hold onto what truly mattered while letting go of what I couldn't carry. This duality—severing and sustaining connections—became part of how I navigated transitions, allowing me to find stability within myself, even when life felt chaotic.

Building Walls to Stay Safe

Years of moving taught me to hold people at arm's length, even as I longed for meaningful connections. People liked me and often wanted to get to know me, and I genuinely desired deep bonds. But I shielded my heart, keeping something back, even in relationships that felt strong and enduring. I maintained connections across the years and miles, but there was always a distance—something unspoken that I allowed to linger between myself and others. I was comfortable with silence and space, perhaps relying too much on the idea that time and distance wouldn't weaken those bonds.

In some ways, I was right. Certain friendships withstood the gaps, the moves, and the silences, holding steady across the seasons of life. This is reflected in my relationship with my longest and dearest friend, my tall Trinidadian dancing queen, who I met during my freshman year of high school in Kaiserslautern, Germany. The two years we lived in Germany are the only years we have ever lived in the same town, yet we've managed over 20 years of laughs, loyalty, and being present for special moments in each other's lives. And then there are the two "Ts," who my parents still get mixed up because their names are so similar and who my children view as aunts. From our daily to weekly late-night laughing, singing our favorite 90s and early 2000s R&B and Hip-Hop songs, and endless talking in dorm rooms with me falling asleep first to our biannual to annual late nights at each other's homes with me still tapping out first. These friendships are steady roots that remind me of where I've been, ground me in who I am, and keep me looking forward to memories we've yet to make.

But not all connections could bear the weight of time apart, and some quietly faded, no matter how much I cared. The abruptness of leaving Germany at 16 had taught me that connections could be fragile, but it also made me hyper-aware of the value of those relationships that could survive the storms. I began to see that even as some bonds faded, others grew stronger because they were rooted in something deeper. That realization stayed with me, shaping the way I approached relationships for years to come.

As I entered my late 30s, though, something began to shift. My children were growing up, becoming more independent, and suddenly, there was a space in my life I hadn't anticipated—a space that longed for connection. I started to feel the pull toward something closer, more present, and more consistent than I'd allowed myself to pursue before. Around this time, "no new friends" was a popular motto, and for a while, it resonated with me. I wasn't necessarily closed off to the idea of new relationships—I had maintained the same best friend from high school and the same close friends from college for over a decade. These friendships had been a source of stability, a testament to the beauty of connection that could withstand distance and time. But even with these enduring bonds, I wasn't actively seeking to expand my circle. My relationships felt "enough," and I told myself I didn't need more.

Still, grace began to nudge at my heart, asking me to reconsider. I started to feel that maybe there was more waiting for me, that maybe I was ready to open myself to something new and deeper. It wasn't about replacing the friendships I cherished—it was about creating space for growth, for connections that might meet me where I was in this new season of life. I knew what it felt like to walk into a new space, to hold back just enough, to never fully be all in, because leaving was always a possibility.

Letting My Roots Grow

One day, a friend from church invited me to join her and her friends, a group I didn't know well. She'd asked before, and I had politely declined each time, holding myself back from making new connections. But this time, I felt something within me shift, and I said, "Yes." That small word became a doorway, opening me up to a circle of women who welcomed me fully.

"Grace is the soil, nourishing our roots and allowing us to flourish, even when we feel exposed."

These friendships were different. They were rooted, consistent, and close. These women saw me as I was without needing me to perform or to protect myself. For the first time in years, I felt myself taking root, trusting that these connections could hold me. Grace was guiding me toward the vulnerability I'd avoided for so long, showing me that strength doesn't come from keeping others at a distance; it comes from letting them close. Like a plant settling into rich, nourishing soil, I began to see that real growth happens when we allow ourselves to be held, seen, and accepted.

These friendships became a daily source of strength. I discovered that connection isn't about showing up perfectly but about showing up fully and sharing the everyday moments that make life whole. Inspired by Thich Nhat Hanh's teachings on mindful communication, I learned to be present with them, to simply be there without needing to fix or solve. Grace taught me that presence was a gift, a reminder that sometimes the most powerful connections are the ones we nurture simply by showing up again and again.

This journey of letting others in allowed me to see that grace is the foundation on which we grow. Grace is the soil, nourishing our roots and allowing us to flourish, even when we feel exposed. In the community, I found strength, realizing that connection doesn't need grand gestures; it just needs consistency, patience, and the courage to be vulnerable.

A Legacy of Roots and Openness

These new friendships opened the door to something even deeper—a connection to my past and to the roots that hold me. I thought of my parents and their marriage of over forty years, a testament to love and resilience. They taught me about commitment, grace, and the importance of showing up. And as a Black woman, I feel the grounding presence of my ancestors. Their legacy of grace and strength runs deep within me, holding me up in ways I can't always see. They remind me that I am part of something larger, connected by history and resilience—I am a part of a village.

Now, as I raise my own family, I see the beauty of passing down these roots, these values of connection and love. Like the deep roots of a tree, our family ties are the lifeblood that nourishes us through every season, grounding us in love and history. Grace has shown me that connection doesn't just hold us—it becomes a legacy passed down to those who come after us. That's the beauty of connection: it endures, transcends, and multiplies.

Whether with family, friends, or even strangers, connection is about more than proximity. It's about the roots we carry within us—the values, love, and strength passed down from one generation to the next. Like trees in a forest, we are connected in ways we often can't see, sharing an invisible network of grace and support. Even when replanted, those original roots remain, guiding us toward connection and growth.

As I reflect on this journey, I realize that opening myself up to connection extends beyond friends and family. Through writing, I am extending my roots even further, creating opportunities to connect with people all over the world—some of whom I may never meet but whose lives I hope to touch. Writing has become a way of opening myself, of letting my voice reach others, of connecting to souls and soil across the world. Whoever once said I was not forthcoming? I am digging, I am open, I am exposed. I am connected.

Grace has taught me that true strength is not in standing alone but in the willingness to be open, to lean on others, and to connect across distances. We are all connected, our roots reaching out, intertwining, and becoming stronger together. Developing in grace means allowing those roots to go deep, trusting that we are held, seen, and nourished by the connections we cultivate, whether close to home or across the world.

 **Stay connected, DIG:**

1. How have certain relationships or communities sustained and nourished you through change?

_____

_____

_____

2. Where might grace invite you to soften walls that protect you from vulnerability?

_____

_____

_____

3. What has being fully present and open in a relationship taught you about trust and connection?

_____

_____

_____

4. What legacy of connection do you hope to create, and how might this extend beyond those close to you?

_____

_____

_____

Continue to DIG

_____

_____

_____

_____

_____

_____

_____

_____

_____

_____

_____

_____

_____

_____

INTERLUDE

"Liberty"

Hear the war cry

Run sprint dance

jump for joy

The Lord is here

People come near

People come from afar

Hurt welcome here

Place of grace

Come get yours

Here for the claiming

Increase your connection

To God, To You

Who knew

How deep one could dive

Hit the floor

Yep, the spirit is strong

Holy Ghost Is Alive

Moving in you

What's the feeling?

Oh, it's Grace flowing all up and through this place

-DIG

CHAPTER 5

Lessons of the Lake

"I do not at all understand the mystery of grace—
only that it meets us where we are but does not
leave us where it found us."

– Anne Lamott

A Leap into the Unknown

We bought our home by the lake at the height of the 2020 pandemic—a time when uncertainty was the only constant. Making an offer on a house sight unseen—on a lake, no less, with small children who couldn't swim—might seem reckless to some, but it was anything but impulsive. The housing market was intense, with homes selling faster than we could blink, often above asking price, and choices in the school district we wanted were slim. Still, there was something about this house, something about the lake, that drew me in. It felt like more than a house; it felt like a place waiting to become part of our lives.

What I didn't fully understand then was just how much we would come to rely on this place—especially in those moments when the outside world felt too chaotic to face. The house on the lake quickly became our home, and the lake itself became my haven—a place of grounding and peace. Each day, I found myself navigating the chaos of homeschooling, work, and everything else from the cove of our cozy home. And yet, just outside my window, the lake was always there. On the busiest, most frantic days, I'd pause and look out over its surface, watching as it reflected light, stillness, and calm back to me.

It felt like a deep exhale—a reminder to slow down, to clear my mind, and to breathe. In a world that felt like it was constantly shifting underfoot, the lake stood steady, offering me quiet strength. It was a space to simply be, to embrace a stillness I hadn't known I needed, even as life swirled relentlessly around me. The lake didn't demand anything of me; it just existed, steadfast and unwavering, inviting me to find my balance amidst the chaos.

The Wonder Beneath

Every now and then, flashes of orange and gold would break through the water's surface—the koi, rising from the depths. Their vibrant colors were unexpected, bright moments of life that reminded me of the beauty hidden below the surface. The koi only appeared when the water was calm, and I realized they reflected grace—grace that often lies hidden, waiting to rise when we least expect it.

The koi became even more meaningful when my best friend, The "Trinidadian dancing queen," visited the lake. She marveled at their beauty and, shortly after, named her daughter and my goddaughter Koi. Now, whenever I think of those koi, I see them not only as symbols of grace and patience but as reminders of how deeply our connections ripple outward, shaping lives in ways we may never fully understand.

Just as the koi surfaced in their own time, life's beauty often reveals itself when we pause long enough to notice. These fish taught me the value of patience and trust—the power of allowing life to unfold naturally rather than rushing to control or force its gifts. Sometimes, we have to DIG deep into the depths of life, embrace its mystery, and wait for its wonders to rise.

The lake taught me to embrace the rhythms of life, mirroring its seasons with my own. Winter brought a frozen stillness, holding everything in quiet suspension. By spring, the ice would melt, and the water would wake, teeming with new life and movement. Summer was full of vibrancy, with fish just beneath the surface, while autumn dressed the lake in golden hues, preparing for rest.

Each season held a lesson about grace. Winter taught me to rest, to let go of constant productivity, and to allow stillness to do its work. Beneath the frozen surface, life doesn't stop; roots grow deeper, storing energy for the seasons ahead. Spring reminded me of the power of renewal, of awakening after the pause. Summer was a time of fullness, a reminder to bask in the abundance of life. Autumn, with its falling leaves and reflective hues, taught me the beauty of release—of trusting that letting go is part of growth.

The trees surrounding our home mirrored this same wisdom. Their roots stretched deep toward the lake, holding them steady even as their branches reached skyward. The trees surrounding our home mirrored this same wisdom. Their roots stretched deep toward the lake, holding them steady even as their branches reached skyward. When I look at the trees planted by the water near our home, I am reminded of the words from Jeremiah 17:7-8 (New International Version): "But blessed is the one who trusts in the Lord, whose confidence is in him. They will be like a tree planted by the water that sends out its roots by the stream. It does not fear when heat comes; its leaves are always green. It has no worries in a year of drought and never fails to bear fruit."

This verse reminds me that, like the trees by the lake, we, too, have become more rooted as a family in this home. Although it wasn't our first choice, being planted here by the water has brought us grounding, beauty, and lessons of grace that we carry with us. Rooted in this grounding, I noticed the life surrounding the lake—the creatures that called it home and the quiet lessons they offered. Each fox slipping through the trees and each crane gliding across the water seemed to remind me of grace in action, resilience, and adaptability.

Creatures and the Creatures We Call Children

One morning, as I sipped my tea and watched the mist rise from the lake, a fox darted across my yard. Its quick, graceful movement caught my eye, and I smiled, marveling at the life that surrounded me. The lake seemed alive with stories—cranes gliding silently across the water, geese landing on the roof with noisy determination, and ducks paddling effortlessly along the surface. Watching them glide across the water, I saw only calm—an image of effortless grace. But beneath the surface, their webbed feet were paddling furiously, working tirelessly to keep them afloat. It reminded me of how people often say, "Candice, you always seem like you have it all together." Like the ducks, I might appear "cool, calm, and copacetic," as my Papa used to say, but beneath the surface, I'm working hard to stay on course.

There's grace in that effort, too—in the unseen work that keeps us moving forward. The ducks taught me that resilience isn't always visible, and the grace we project to the world doesn't diminish the hard work beneath the surface. It's all part of the same story—the story of staying afloat in a world that often feels overwhelming.

These lessons of grace extended to my children. The lake became a place of grounding for them as well, teaching them to trust the shallow waters in our cove. "If you fall in, just stand up," I'd tell them. One day, my son slipped in, only to pop back up, laughing. "See, Mom? It's not that deep. I just stood up, and I'm okay!" he said, echoing the very words I'd taught him.

"...the roots we establish are what allow us to reach out, to grow, and to take risks."

Over time, they grew bolder, venturing into deeper waters and learning to swim and trust themselves. The lake became their teacher, showing them that life has its depths but also its grounding points. They were learning, just like me, that the roots we establish are what allow us to reach out, to grow, and to take risks.

Grace in Every Change

Living by the lake has taught me that grace is both constant and mysterious. It's in the quiet presence of something steady, in the cycles that ground us, and in the roots that hold us. Grace isn't about perfect balance or mastering life's chaos—it's about finding strength in the things that remain, even as everything else shifts.

Sitting by the water, I learned I didn't need to control every wave or anticipate every change. Like the lake, I could DIG deep, hold my ground, and trust that grace would meet me exactly where I was. The lake reminded me that peace doesn't come from perfection; it comes from presence. Can you please explain what presence means in this sentence?

It's about noticing the stillness beneath life's movements and finding steadiness within yourself. Presence allows you to pause, breathe, and recognize the beauty in what is steady and enduring, even in the midst of life's uncertainties. The lake is a gentle reminder that grace doesn't demand action; it simply invites you to be present, to rest in the now, and to trust in the strength of your roots.

 ## Go with the flow, DIG:

1. What parts of your life feel like "frantic paddling" beneath the surface? How can you find grace in that hidden work?

_____

_____

_____

2. How can you trust in the roots you've already planted, even as life calls you into new transitions?

_____

_____

_____

3. In what ways can you honor the cycles in your life, letting each season bring its own growth without rushing through?

_____

_____

_____

Continue to DIG

_____

_____

_____

_____

_____

_____

_____

_____

_____

_____

_____

_____

_____

_____

INTERLUDE

Issa Process

Issa a process

Trust the process

Healing inside of me

What's the process

Restoration

Deliverance is key

Breathe in, breathe out

Don't stop

Stay rooted

Live life

Keep all in perspective

This task is bigger than me.

God's grace.

We all have yet to see

God's grace

Sufficient for all

Issa a process

Trust the process

Healing inside of you

-DIG

CHAPTER 6

Strength Redefined by Grace

"Grace is not weakness; it is strength beyond measure."
– Jackie Robinson

The words lingered longer than I wanted them to: *"You've got the body of a 60-year-old woman."* My chiropractor didn't realize how his casual comment, meant as an observation, would settle into the soil of my thoughts. For years, I had leaned on my body as a reliable partner, trusting it to keep up with the demands of my life. From carrying the weight of my family's needs to navigating the stress of work and the quiet burden of societal expectations, I thought I was holding everything together. But now, the wear and tear told a different story.

The truth was, I had stretched myself too thin—physically, emotionally, and mentally. The strain I carried in one area bled into the others, and my body had been keeping the score. I hadn't realized how much I had asked of myself until my body finally said *enough*. It was like hearing that my garden, my plot of land, had withered from neglect. And it broke my heart.

The shame came quickly, carrying with it the weight of reflection. I thought of all the moments when I would have listened, could have made different choices, and should have cared more for myself. But I didn't. Instead, I pushed through, ignoring the whispers of my body until they became shouts.

For someone who prided herself on having no regrets, this moment tested me. I wasn't just reckoning with my body breaking down; I was reckoning with the choices that led me here. Yet, as I've come to understand, growth doesn't happen in a straight line. Growth can be difficult and uncomfortable, like roots breaking through hardened soil or a tree bending under the weight of the wind. For a girl raised to believe that strength meant never bending, never breaking, this reckoning demanded profound transformation because the would have, could have, and should have in my mind were closing in on me.

The Would Haves:

In 2014, my body began speaking to me quietly at first. Childbirth and the weight of mothering, along with everything else, changed me—physically, emotionally, and mentally. What once felt strong and steady now felt fragile, requiring care and attention. The physical shifts—from back pain to changes in my hips, feet, knees, pelvic floor—you name it (in my Shirley Caesar voice) were constant reminders that my body was no longer the same.

Mentally and emotionally, I remember that the only thing clear to me was that I was done birthing children. Growing up as one of five siblings, I had shared in caretaking for my younger brothers and sisters. I thought I could handle having the same number of children. But the two I birthed, along with my bonus daughter, proved to be more than enough. I was shocked at how clearly my body, mind, and emotions told me I could not handle more.

Once again, judgment flooded in. *What's wrong with me?* My mother had raised five children with what seemed like ease and nurture. I told myself I should be able to do the same. The weight of the *would have, should have, could have* bore down on me heavier than ever.

Looking back, I realize I would have listened earlier if I hadn't been so consumed with proving my strength. There were signs and moments when my body tried to tell me to slow down, to rest, to heal. But I ignored them. I convinced myself that strength meant endurance and that everything would be fine if I could just hold on a little longer.

Yoga became my lifeline during that time. It gave me space to stretch and breathe, to feel my body without judgment. I often found myself practicing tree pose, one foot rooted firmly to the ground while the other rested gently against my leg, my arms reaching toward the sky. That pose, balancing strength and reach, mirrored what I longed for in life: stability and growth. For the first time in years, I experienced moments of stillness, moments when I wasn't trying to prove anything.

But as life became more demanding, I let yoga slip away. I told myself I didn't have time, even though I knew it was what I needed most. If I had understood the value of that softness, I might have anchored myself in it. Instead, I returned to what I knew—pushing harder, carrying more, and holding everything together.

The Could Haves:

"Growth can be difficult and uncomfortable, like roots breaking through hardened soil..."

Then life piled on. Justin lost his job. Around the same time, I was promoted to a managerial role that demanded more from me than I was prepared to give. Suddenly, I found myself carrying the weight of our family's well-being. It wasn't just financial—it was emotional. My new role came with daily microaggressions and unconscious biases from colleagues who couldn't reconcile a young Black woman as their superior. At home, I faced the high needs of my children, born to anxious parents still carrying unresolved trauma that manifested in their own behaviors and anxiety. I could have paused. I could have asked for help. But instead, I convinced myself that it was my job to handle it all. Resentment began to take root, growing like weeds in the spaces where I needed grace. My life felt unbalanced, and my body and relationships mirrored that imbalance.

The Should Haves:

The tension I carried wasn't just emotional—it was physical. I became so tense that even a hug felt overwhelming. My body stiffened at every touch, holding stress like an overfilled container ready to burst. That tension seeped into every aspect of my life. In my marriage, where my husband's love language was physical touch, I found myself unable to give love in the way he needed. My own body's rigidity became a barrier between us, and no amount of good intentions could bridge that gap.

The tension also found its way into my relationships with my children. I remember my mom telling me that my son had described me as *harsh*. I was taken aback—not only by the word itself, which felt far too mature for his budding vocabulary—but by how accurate it was. I couldn't deny it. My stress and strain were showing up in my parenting, leaving little room for softness or nurture. Even my relationship with myself felt distant, as though I were a stranger navigating my own body and emotions.

I should have recognized sooner that the way I was moving through life wasn't sustainable. As sure as the snap I heard in my foot one day, my life had snapped, crackled, and popped. And unlike the cereal, it wasn't good. My body was giving out under the weight I carried, and my soul felt as dry and thirsting as soil during a drought. My flowers were wilting, neglected, and withering from the inside out.

But here's the thing about brokenness: it creates space for light to pour in. Grace was waiting for me in the cracks, ready to transform my dry soil into something fertile again.

The Weight We Carry:

As a Black woman, the weight I carried wasn't just personal—it was generational and societal. I remember sitting in my *Psychology of Oppression* class in college, playing Monopoly to simulate socioeconomic inequality. By the end of the game, a white classmate who had lost all her money and property said, *"I feel like the poorest Black woman ever."*

Her unconscious bias was on full display. She believed the poorest Black woman was the lowest, most pitiable state anyone could experience. I remember sitting there, thinking: *I am a woman, I am Black, and as a college student surviving on little, I am poor. In her eyes, I am the worst thing one could be.*

That realization stayed with me. The weight of existing in a world where my strength had to be superhuman to simply survive was overwhelming. I fought against microaggressions at work, carried the pressures of being "strong" at home, and battled the unspoken expectation that I should carry all of this without breaking. How does one remain soft in that? *Grace.*

All of the would-have, could-have, and should-haves and the weight required a newer approach. I had spent so many years striving for perfection, trying to do everything right, and being strong for everyone around me. Grace reminded me that I didn't have to be perfect. I could rest, I could fail, and I could still be strong. This shift transformed my life, especially in my marriage and family. For so long, I carried so much weight—physically, emotionally, and mentally—believing that was what a strong woman, wife, and mother did. But as I began to soften, I discovered that strength wasn't about how much I could carry. It was about how much I could allow myself to release.

Thriving Through Grace:

For years, I believed strength meant pushing through. But now, I see strength in softness. Like a tree rooted deeply in the earth, I've learned to bend with the wind, not against it. My roots anchor me, giving me stability, while my branches stretch toward the sky, flexible and reaching for growth. Tree pose reminds me of this balance: rooted in strength, yet reaching with grace.

I am both strong and soft. I am rooted and growing.

This redefinition didn't come easily. I had to unlearn rigid beliefs that once shaped me. I replaced my *Survival Music* playlist with *Thrive Music*, locking in my new goal: thriving, not surviving.

My workouts shifted, too. High-impact boot camps gave way to yoga and walking. I began each morning with a green drink—kale or spinach blended into something that nourished me from the inside out. Ginger, turmeric, cayenne pepper, vegetables, and water became staples as I embraced food as medicine. These weren't just acts of recovery; they were celebrations of care, acts of self-compassion that reflected my growth.

There's a part of me—an old soul connected to the wiser, calmer version of myself—that whispers to me when I'm doing too much. Nowadays, the kids say, "You're doing too much," often completely out of context—such as when I simply ask them to clean up after themselves. But when my body starts signaling that I'm genuinely doing too much, that old-soul voice steps in, saying, "You better sit down before you get sat down."

I believe my body is my temple, and my work in hospice has shown me just how fragile our bodies and lives can be. That phrase has become my way of honoring the vessel I've been given. It's part humor, part survival mantra, and entirely necessary. Saying it aloud to myself—or even to others—is my gentle reminder to pause, breathe, and care for the body that carries me through this life. Speaking of new mantras...

I am learning to embrace ease, seek peace, and find joy in life's softness. In *The Color Purple*, Sophia (Oprah's character) says, *"All my life, I had to fight."* My new motto is different: *"All my life, I'm not going to fight."* Grace has taught me that I don't have to live in survival mode. I can thrive in softness or, as the younger generation of women calls it—my soft girl era.

I am strong, and I am soft. I am not one or the other—I am both. That's what true strength is: the ability to hold the tension between strength and softness, between roots and branches, between survival and grace.

 ## You are soft and strong, you can DIG:

1. How has your understanding of strength evolved over time?

_____

_____

_____

2. In what areas of your life do you need to redefine what it means to be strong?

_____

_____

_____

3. How can grace help you embrace a new definition of strength that honors your body, mind, and spirit?

_____

_____

_____

Continue to DIG

_____

_____

_____

_____

_____

_____

_____

_____

_____

_____

_____

_____

_____

_____

_____

_____

Fly Like a Butterfly, Swat Like a Ninja

There was a time when I worked under a supervisor who struggled with micromanaging. It seemed like every task I completed, and every decision I made was met with a barrage of questions. To me, it felt like she was constantly doubting my abilities, questioning my competence at every turn. The frustration grew as I found myself needing to defend every move I made, every choice I took. It was exhausting, and I started to feel like I was being pushed to my limits.

"...learning to embrace ease, seek peace and to find joy in life's softness."

To cope, I began writing notes to myself, little coded messages that only I could understand. They became my way of staying grounded amidst the chaos. One of these notes quickly became my mantra:

Fly like a butterfly. Swat like a ninja. Sit like a frog. No sting like a bee.

This simple phrase carried deep meaning for me. It was a reminder to float away from issues that weren't mine and not get stuck in the frustrations surrounding me. I told myself to swat away problems that didn't belong to me, to seize what was mine to handle, and let go of the rest. I reminded myself to sit still and not react to every challenge that came my way. And, most importantly, I told myself not to sting—not to lash out in anger, even when I felt cornered. It was my way of keeping grace close, even when everything around me felt overwhelming.

This mantra helped me navigate the difficult dynamics with my supervisor. It became my shield against the stress and frustration that came with her micromanagement. I kept that note in my office, a constant reminder to stay true to myself, to hold on to my grace.

As time passed, something unexpected happened. I began to see things differently. Through grace, I started to understand that my supervisor's questions weren't about me at all. She wasn't questioning my abilities or trying to undermine my work. Instead, she was seeking understanding for herself. Her questions were her way of processing the work and ensuring she could provide the support we needed.

Once I saw this, our working relationship began to shift. I stopped feeling so defensive and stopped seeing her as an adversary. Instead, I began to extend the same grace to her that I was giving myself. I realized that she, too, was doing the best she could, and her micromanaging was more about her own insecurities than about any lack of trust in me.

Now, that note hangs in my new office at my new job. It's more than just a memory of how I navigated that challenging time; it's a reminder I use not just at work but in my personal and professional life, too. It's signed *DIG*, my constant reminder to develop in grace, to find peace in the midst of challenges, and to express myself, even when the world tries to push me in a different direction.

So, what's your coded message? How do you keep grace close when people need you? For me, it's *DIG*—developing in grace and allowing myself the space to handle life's complexities with care and understanding.

CHAPTER 7

Developing Grace:
A Continuous Journey

"Grace now means that all of your mistakes now serve a purpose instead of serving a shame."

– Brene Brown.

Grace has always been an evolving concept in my life, a journey that has deepened with each passing year. In the early stages of my personal and professional growth, I was consumed by the need to constantly improve myself—reading books, attending seminars, and looking for the next big idea that would somehow make me feel complete. I believed that if I could just gather enough information and refine my abilities enough, I would finally reach a place of peace and fulfillment.

But the truth is, this endless pursuit often felt like walking a winding road filled with detours and distractions. There was always another self-help book to read, another podcast to listen to, another course to take. I found myself constantly comparing my progress to others, feeling envious of their achievements, and questioning why I wasn't further along on my own path. I also wrestled with thoughts like *I did everything right—I made good choices, I was obedient, I graduated high school and college, got married, waited until marriage to have kids, and worked hard.* These comparisons and endless pursuits of perfectionism became barriers on my journey, pulling me away from the grace that was always available to me.

Growing Into Grace

I have had to grow into the recognition of grace as a continuous and ever-present part of my life. I've often found myself

"Grace doesn't take away disappointment or erase hardship, it softens the edges."

wanting to reach certain milestones or "arrivals" in my life. For example, I thought that once I reached a particular point, everything would fall into place. When I was single, I hoped for the day I'd get married, thinking the love of my partner would complete what felt unfinished. Once married, I looked forward to having children. When my children came, I believed a sense of fulfillment and purpose would steady my restless soul. Instead, I placed a new set of pressures on myself and my children. I found myself striving to be a certain kind of wife and mother. During those times, grace seemed like a foreign language. Even in friendships, I often held expectations of how I wanted to be treated or valued, hoping for predictability, comfort, and loyalty. All the while forgetting at times that people be peopling.

This constant pursuit of "arriving" has often kept me in a state of striving, looking for fulfillment just around the corner, always expecting a certain outcome. But grace has shown me that life's journey—especially in relationships—is not about reaching an endpoint. The notion of arriving is just that, a notion. Each milestone I reached revealed new challenges, new uncertainties, and a deeper need for surrender. Learning that grace isn't the reward for reaching a destination has been a humbling process.

When I think about what has to be "dug" in this process, I realize that developing in grace means allowing ourselves to dig deeper into understanding, patience, and acceptance. It means releasing the rigid expectations we may place on ourselves and others and instead being curious about who they are, where they are, and what they bring to our lives. Grace invites me to see each relationship as an ongoing journey, one that doesn't need a fixed destination to have meaning.

Working in hospice taught me a profound lesson about this. Each time I left a visit with a patient, I would say, "I'm on to my next adventure," never quite knowing what the next encounter would hold. Reflecting, I realize that during that time, I was learning about grace without even recognizing it. I was learning that even though I didn't know what each outcome would be, I could find peace in the moment, allowing the lessons, the breaths, and the connections to come in their own time. I had to be open to each new encounter, accepting that every patient, every story, and every moment held something unique.

This openness has translated into my relationships over time. Grace has shown me that being curious and receptive to others—whether it's my spouse, children, friends, or colleagues—means making space for who they truly are rather than who I expect or hope them to be. For someone who struggles with perfectionism, self-criticism, and shame, curiosity provides the necessary space between judgment and reactivity that had become second nature to me. Developing in grace means digging deeper into compassion and understanding, letting each interaction be part of the journey rather than a means to an end.

Acknowledging Life's Challenges

Life is full of challenges—losing a sense of stability when you least expect it, the pain of a friendship that has run its course, the strain of family relationships, the sting of unmet goals, the disappointment of losing out on something you deeply hoped for, and even the profound sorrow of losing someone you love. These moments can make you question everything—your choices, your worth, your direction, and sometimes even life itself. They can cloud your path, making the way forward seem unclear and the destination unreachable.

I often return to my years working in hospice, reflecting on one of the most rewarding and challenging roles I've ever held: facilitating grief groups in Louisville Public Schools. As a School-Based Grief Counselor, I worked with small groups of students who had experienced a loss due to death. Over six weeks, we created a space to explore the complex emotions of grief, learn about death and dying, develop healthy ways of coping, and find ways to adjust to life without their loved ones.

These sessions were a powerful reminder of how grief, like grace, is not something that ends but evolves with us over time.

In our final session, we concluded with an activity called the Rough Rock ceremony. It was a beautiful and meaningful way to help the students reflect on their grief journey. Closure is often mentioned in discussions of grief, but I've learned that grief, much like grace, does not have a definitive endpoint. As long as we live, we will grieve in one way or another those we have loved and lost. And as long as we live, we will continue to evolve in grace.

The Rough Rock ceremony encapsulates this ongoing process. Each object used in the activity symbolized a part of the grief journey, illustrating how pain and loss can be transformed into something meaningful. The **rough rock** represented the jagged, raw pain of loss, the overwhelming hurt that felt impossible to bear in the beginning. With time and reflection, this pain can become less sharp, its edges softened like a **smooth stone** polished by the steady flow of a river. In much the same way, grace works in our lives to gently transform our struggles,

125

smoothing the rough edges and allowing us to move forward with a renewed sense of purpose.

The ceremony also included a **pipe cleaner person**, which symbolized the enduring presence of our loved ones. Even though they are no longer physically with us, their impact remains woven into our story. The **rubber band** served as a reminder of resilience, teaching us that while we may stretch and bend under the weight of our grief, we do not have to break. The **penny**, with its two sides, symbolized the duality of grief— the pain of what was lost and the hope of what remains. And finally, the **feather** represented the lightness that can come with time. What feels unbearably heavy in the beginning may one day become lighter to carry, like a feather that floats gently on the wind.

As I reflect on this activity, I see how it mirrors the journey of developing in grace. Life's challenges often begin as jagged and overwhelming, but grace invites us to allow these moments to shape us rather than define us. Just as the river smooths the rough rock, grace works quietly and persistently to transform our pain into strength and growth.

The Rough Rock ceremony is a profound reminder that grace is always present, even in life's hardest moments. It teaches us to embrace the transformation process and trust that, over time, what feels unbearable can evolve into something meaningful. And it reminds us that, just like grace, grief is not a destination but a continuous journey—one that invites us to carry both the weight of our loss and the lightness of our growth hand in hand.

Reflecting on this activity, I see how it mirrors the journey of developing in grace. Life's challenges may begin as jagged and overwhelming, but grace shows us that, over time, these moments can shape us into something smoother, something stronger. The lessons from the Rough Rock ceremony remind me that grace is present even in the hardest moments, gently working to transform pain into growth.

In these times, I've come to see grace as a root system that keeps me grounded through life's "droughts" and "storms." Each challenge—strained relationships, disappointments, and loss—

is a test of resilience, a reminder to dig deeper, drawing strength from a place beyond what is visible on the surface. Grace has taught me that even when the soil is rocky or dry, I can find nourishment and grounding by turning inward and relying on a wellspring of strength that grace has grown within me over time.

This grounding has been especially important in moments of grief. One thing I often told those I worked with as a grief counselor was to *be gentle with themselves and their grief process.* Grief, like grace, is not linear—it ebbs and flows, softening at times and surging at others. It requires patience, understanding, and, most of all, grace. Grace reminds us to tread lightly, offer ourselves and others compassion, and recognize that healing is not about perfection but presence. Just as roots find a way to grow through rocky soil, grace allows us to continue even when the path feels impossible.

"Grace is like the earth itself-stable, grounding, yet constantly renewing."

I know these challenges all too well. When facing life's setbacks, it's easy to feel lost, to doubt the path you're on, and to wonder if all the effort has been in vain. But grace has a way of showing up during these struggles, offering a hand to steady us. Grace doesn't take away disappointment or erase hardship; it softens the edges. It's the presence that reminds me to breathe, to accept the twists and turns as part of the journey, and to keep moving forward, even if I can't see the destination.

When I'm up against life's challenges, I've learned that grace is essential not only toward myself but also toward others. There have been times in parenting, marriage, relationships, and the workplace when I withheld grace, and the effects were undeniable. Without grace, I found myself stuck in cycles of disappointment, anger, hurt, and numbness, feeling distant and checked out. By not extending grace, I stayed locked in my own frustrations and expectations, unable to move forward.

"Grace invites us to keep moving forward, to trust the journey, and to embrace the beauty of the path we're on..."

In my family relationships, I've encountered moments of strain that felt like barriers I couldn't get past. There were times when conversations left wounds instead of healing, times when misunderstandings grew into walls. Grace has taught me to approach these moments differently. Instead of closing off or shutting down, I've learned to pause and extend grace—to myself and to others. It's a gentle reminder that even when relationships falter, there is room for understanding, patience, and forgiveness. Grace allows us to move forward, to try again, and to keep the connection alive, even when it's not easy.

The Continuous Evolution of Grace

Ultimately, grace is like the earth itself—stable, grounding, yet constantly renewing. Just as roots dig into the soil for stability and nourishment, grace reaches deep within me, anchoring and sustaining us even when life's storms shake everything on the surface. Every challenge, every relationship, and every new stage in life brings with it an opportunity to expand, to draw even closer to this source of strength.

Grace is not a final destination; it's the ever-deepening root system that strengthens and grows with me as I continue forward. With each experience, I draw from it, nourish it, and let it reshape me. It's the quiet reassurance that we are always on the path, even when we encounter distractions or barriers. Grace invites us to keep moving forward, to trust in the journey, and to embrace the beauty of the path we're on—detours, droughts, disappointments, and all. And like any journey, what sustains us is not just the movement forward but the strength of what lies beneath—our roots. Deep, unseen, yet always anchoring us.

As you continue reading, I invite you to stay open to the ways grace may meet you along the way. Let go of the need to arrive or to achieve some final understanding. Instead, let this journey be one of curiosity, discovery, and acceptance. Grace is there to catch you, to guide you, and to root you deeply exactly where you need to be.

 **Try on this different version of strength I call DIG:**

1. Where in your relationships are you holding onto expectations, and how can grace help you let go?

_____

_____

_____

2. What would it look like to embrace grace as an ongoing journey rather than a destination?

_____

_____

_____

3. How has grace shown up for you in challenging moments, and how can you welcome it more often?

_____

_____

_____

4. How can you stay open to grace meeting you exactly where you are?

_____

_____

_____

Continue to DIG

_____

_____

_____

_____

_____

_____

_____

_____

_____

_____

_____

_____

_____

_____

_____

_____

_____

Lazy Rivers and Grace

I have always loved a lazy river. There's something about the gentle, rhythmic flow that feels like an invitation to let go and trust the current. I've been known to drift off to sleep, rocked by the steady movement of the water, completely at peace. Unlike the unpredictable rapids of life, the lazy river is a place of ease and surrender. Sure, there are occasional splashes—maybe a small waterfall you can avoid, or maybe not—but the river keeps flowing. You can get on and off at will, pause for play, for conversation, for stillness. There are no crocodiles here, no lurking dangers—only the reassurance that the river will carry you forward in its own time.

Grace, I've learned, is a lot like that. It is the steady force that moves us, catches us, and carries us forward when we stop striving and trust its flow. This activity invites you to create your own Lazy River of Grace—a space where you can reflect on the rhythm of your journey and embrace the beauty of floating, resting, and trusting the process.

Imagine stepping into a gentle, winding, lazy river—your own personal flow of grace. The water moves at just the right pace, carrying you effortlessly forward. You don't have to paddle or struggle; the river knows the way. Along the journey, you might pass peaceful moments, joyful gatherings, places of rest, or unexpected splashes of challenge—but you always have the choice to stay in the flow or step off and explore.

Activity: Designing Your Own Lazy River of Grace

Step 1: Visualize Your River

Close your eyes and imagine your own lazy river. What does the water feel like? What sounds surround you? What emotions rise as you float?

Step 2: Identify What's Along Your Path

- Where do you stop for joy, connection, and play?
- Where do you pause for stillness and reflection?
- What unexpected waterfalls or splashes might you encounter? How do you handle them?
- What anchors you in grace when you're in the flow?

Step 3: Journal or Draw Your River

Sketch out your lazy river, marking the places where grace, joy, rest, and challenges appear along the way. If you prefer writing, describe your journey—what moments are the most healing? Where do you feel most at ease?

Step 4: Embrace the Flow

Take a deep breath. Recognize that grace is a continuous journey—one where you can always return to the river, float at your own pace, and trust that the current will carry you exactly where you need to go.

Closing Reflection:

Grace is not about forcing the flow; it's about trusting that the river knows the way. May you be open to developing in grace, allowing yourself to float, to rest, to play, and to trust the journey ahead. **– DIG**

CHAPTER 8

Roots That Run Deep

"A tree with strong roots laughs at storms."
– Malay Proverb

Roots of Storytelling

Storytelling was the main event in my grandparent's home. My Grandma, whom most called "Bobbie," raised ten of her own children—plus was a caretaker for countless family members and neighborhood children—making her and my grandfather's modest two-bedroom house in St. Louis, MO, a haven. Sitting at her feet as a child, I heard stories so wild I thought they couldn't possibly be true. Yet as I grew older, lived more life, and felt the weight of experience, I began to understand that every one of her words held a deep, unshakable truth. POWERFUL!!

One of my favorite stories was about a trip down to Mississippi to bring my grandfather back home. Yes, that's all I'll say. Y'all paid for a part of my life story, not every juicy detail. Picture this: she showed up in Mississippi with a Bible in one hand and a pistol in the other. Needless to say, my Papa made it back home to St. Louis safe and sound. That was my grandmother— fiercely loyal, unafraid to carry her faith and fire wherever life led her. In our family, even imperfect marriages found their way back to the roots of what was best for the family. Sometimes, those roots led one down south, packing both faith and fire, but they always returned with resolve and a commitment to the family's legacy.

In times when my own marriage has faced storms, I have found myself packing my own kind of faith and fire, digging deep into the same roots that carried my grandparents and parents through trials. Like them, I've learned that there's strength in staying grounded, even when it's difficult, and that sometimes, the roots of marriage require tending, pruning, and, above all, faith.

On my father's side, there were stories about my Big Daddy. You might think that a name like that belonged to a man of large stature, but let me tell you, the only thing big on him—besides his hair (just picture Don King's hair)—was the respect he commanded. As the oldest of a large family, he shouldered the weight of supporting those who came behind him. Every family gathering brought another retelling of how "nobody better 'f' with AJ Williams." In our family, we had a word for people like him: "notoratic."

Now, "notoratic" may not be in any dictionary, but for us, it was as real as anything else. It described a kind of wild, bold spirit. I grew up thinking it was a universal word, only to find out in my thirties that it wasn't. I'd used it at work, and everyone around me stared like I'd just made it up. A quick internet search confirmed it was not of the Queen's English. But to me—and to my family—that word was real. So rooted in our DNA that when I went back to my parents and told them it didn't officially exist, they didn't believe me. All I could do was laugh. Notaratic is ours, part of the unspoken language of our roots.

Growing up in a family like mine meant living among storytellers, each tale woven with truth and imagination, creating a bond that drew us closer together. There's something about hearing someone else's story that lets you feel your own and others' humanity intertwined. Maybe that's why I'm able to sit with stories as a therapist, letting others lay down their burdens through words. I've been listening to stories since I was a little girl—stories that at times felt bigger than my little body could hold, yet somehow, I could always make space.

On holidays, you could wander from room to room, each one alive with the hum of voices and laughter, listening to stories of days gone by. But these weren't just distant memories—they were told with such vivid detail it felt as if you were stepping back into the moment with them. I didn't just hear these stories once; I heard them over and over, each retelling planting them deeper in my memory, like roots anchoring themselves for safekeeping. Pictures might capture a moment or a thousand words, but stories hold something greater. They carry the threads that weave us together, guiding us back to where we come from and keeping us connected to and reflective of each other.

Those early stories became my first introduction to the power of oral traditions—the ability to carry history, culture, and identity through storytelling. Years later, as a student at Saint Louis University, I found myself yearning for more connections to stories that felt like my own. Attending a predominantly white institution, I was often surrounded by teachings and narratives about people who didn't look like me. To bridge that gap, I pursued a certificate in African American Studies alongside my Bachelor's in Psychology. Those classes, particularly with Professor Witherspoon and Dr. Scott, became a way to reconnect with my roots and would also become a part of my own storytelling.

"...resilience isn't just about enduring—it's about choosing joy, finding release, and letting the light in even during life's darkest moments."

I'll never forget one particular day when my then-boyfriend (now husband) walked me to class. He didn't attend the university, but he loved being near me as much as possible— something that hasn't changed to this day. As we approached the classroom, my professor's booming voice rang out, "Justin, what you doing here, boy?" It turns out that my professor was like family to Justin—a 'play uncle,' as we say in our culture. Instead of just dropping me off, Justin was invited to stay for class, and afterward, they shared stories of old. Moments like these reminded me that stories connect us in ways we can't always anticipate.

In another African American Studies course taught by a Black woman professor, whom I adored and found great comfort in seeing many parts of who I was becoming reflected back, I learned about Jack and Jill of America, an organization founded by visionary mothers during segregation to nurture their children's sense of self-worth and leadership. Even before I became a mother, I was drawn to their story of legacy and vision. I believe that understanding your past helps to shape your future. As I write this book, that belief resonates deeply, reflected in my role as the Program Director for the East St. Louis chapter of Jack and Jill of America, Inc. As I reflect on the seeds those women planted in 1938, I see the deep roots of their work and the abundant harvest it has produced—262 chapters representing over 50,000 families. I am honored to have heard the story of our founding mothers and to carry their mission forward. Their story, like so many others I encountered during those courses, kept me rooted in a time when I needed to feel connected beyond what I saw.

Laughter, Resilience, and Connection

My roots, you see, I come from generations of deeply rooted people—no shallow soil here. As I write, I laugh to myself about recently playing a game with friends called "Stir the Pot." I told y'all earlier about me, gameplay, and the turn it can take. In this game, you pull a card and choose who in the group is most representative of the card. For example, a card might say who in the group most like You, then flip a coin to either tell or don't what the card said. Messy, I know, and disclaimer: I would not recommend it in certain groups or with untamed dragons. Anyways, one of my friends landed on tell, and to my dismay, she chose me as the shallowest of the group. I felt a certain way after hearing that and wrestled a little bit with it, but as I sit here writing about no shallow soil here and how my roots run deep, I recognize the esteem I carry myself with. I recognize the love of self and the protection of self. I remember thinking oh, she doesn't really know me- not fully. It's not her fault; my roots run deep, deeper than most can see. I'm reflective that people often see others, myself included, like a flower in bloom — what's visible on the surface is all they think there is. But like any plant, the beauty above ground is only part of the story. My roots run deep, stretching far beneath the surface, holding seen and unseen layers of strength, faith, and history. It takes more to get to truly know me because the richest parts of who I am lie beneath.

This depth is reflected in my family's faith, which runs through our lives like a river that never dries. I come from a lineage of large family systems—my grandparents had many children, and they made faith the cornerstone of our lives. My family wasn't deeply religious in a strict sense, but belief in God had space to take root in a

"Legacy is like tending a tree—nurturing its roots, honoring the strength of its trunk, and shaping its branches to grow with purpose."

flexible, nurturing way. Prayer was a constant, church a fixture, but the principle of love and, as they say now, family over everything was central. Their legacy wasn't just in the homes they built or the stories they told; it was in the covenant of marriage that each generation carried forward. Banning Liebscher speaks to this in *Rooted: The Hidden Places Where God*

Develops You, describing how God's purpose for us is revealed over time, like roots growing deeper with each passing year. Each marriage, each generation, is a testimony to that faith. The roots of my family run deep because they were nourished by faith, by promises kept, by commitments, and by stories that could bring you to tears from the pain of struggle or, more often, from the laughter that withstood life's storms.

I have learned to dig into laughter, to pray, and to laugh even more. Humor is an essential part of my personality, and it shows up in so many ways—from laughing at myself when I could cry to finding creative ways to confront conflict and navigate crucial conversations. Humor also helps me manage my own "dragon," that fierce, protective part of me that can flare up when I feel threatened or overwhelmed. Without humor, that dragon might look more like *Drogon* from *Game of Thrones*—fiery, intense, and ready to scorch the nearest obstacle. But laughter allows me to soften those moments, to keep the fire in check, and to let *Puff the Magic Dragon* show up instead—a lighter, gentler version of strength that can disarm tension without destruction.

Humor gives me the ability to communicate hard truths or navigate sensitive topics with care. As a clinician, I've conducted countless assessments—suicide, grief, resource needs, you name it—and I've often found that a person's ability to engage in humor reveals their resilience, their perspective, and their capacity for strength. Humor, to me, is more than just a coping mechanism. It's ancient wisdom passed down, a way to hold space for struggle while still finding light. It's the balance between levity and gravity, a tool that reminds me to stay connected to grace, even in the hardest moments.

I operate in the world guided by a sense of awareness deeply rooted in family, faith, and the unseen knowledge of my ancestors. These roots ground me, allowing me to navigate life with humor, intention, and an appreciation for both the lighthearted *Puff* moments and the fiery strength of my dragon when needed.

DIG-ing Into Legacy

As I reflect on where this balance comes from, I realize much of it is rooted in the example set by my mother. She's always had a knack for making people feel welcome and drawing people to her. My friends have always easily connected and adamantly requested to be adopted as another daughter. Her gifts go beyond words; they're about connection. She has a gift for gathering people, feeding both body and soul, and making anyone who enters her home feel like family. Toward the end of her mother's life, my mother came to a profound realization—not only did she share her mother's namesake and the ability to raise a large family, but she also carried the same gifts that defined my grandmother. They were both connectors, caregivers, and fiercely loyal women who could whip a meal from scratch out of almost nothing and create a legacy of family that was entirely their own. The families they built were bonded by a strength and love that ran deeper than blood, a connection that looked like no one else's but ours.

My grandmother had a way of sharing her life's stories that left an indelible mark on all of us. She would smile, her eyes twinkling, and tell her stories—not with tears, but with laughter so full it seemed to shake the room. Her laugh was a lesson in itself, showing us that we can go through trying times without letting them harden us. Instead, her laugh broke down walls, softened hearts, and dissolved tension with the ease of a good, old-fashioned belly laugh. She showed us that resilience isn't just about enduring—it's about choosing joy, finding release, and letting the light in even during life's darkest moments.

Watching my mother live this out showed me that her ability to unite us through story, laughter, and shared meals was a direct extension of the roots she came from. And as her mother's life drew to a close, it became clear just how deeply these roots ran. Some gifts, like roots, become more visible the longer they grow. And some roots—those gifts of warmth, humor, and connection—are there from the beginning, needing only time to blossom fully.

Roots are curious things. They are often hidden, unseen, growing beneath the surface. But in those depths, they are fiercely alive. In trees, the roots grow far beyond what you can see above ground—sometimes stretching several times wider than the branches, silently working, holding strong. They break through rocks, curve around obstacles, and search for nutrients in the soil, finding ways to thrive even in the harshest conditions. Roots aren't merely anchoring a tree or plant; they are seeking, pushing, and digging deep for life.

My papa always said, "Ain't nothing shaking but the leaves on the trees, and they wouldn't shake if it wasn't for the breeze."

"Just as soil needs to be tilled, watered, and cared for, so too do we need to tend to our inner selves."

His words remind me that while roots hold us steady, life's unseen forces—the breeze—move us, shaping and strengthening us. It's in that movement that we find resilience and grace, carried forward by forces we don't always see but deeply feel. The roots keep us grounded, but the breeze reminds us to adapt, stretch, and grow.

There's something else that roots do—they communicate. They share nutrients and warnings, and they pass wisdom through the ground, not just for their own survival but for the whole forest. Our roots, too, are filled with stories and lessons that become our family's nourishment, our connection.

Just as a tree with deep roots can withstand storms, a family rooted in stories, shared truths, enduring faith, unconditional love, and heartfelt laughter can withstand life's trials. When we pass down our history, we pass down a kind of shield, a source of strength. My grandmother's laughter and my mother's stories aren't just memories; they're the water and sunlight that our roots needed to DIG deeper and stay grounded. And laughter, I've found, is perhaps the greatest nourishment of all. It's the salve for the scars that life leaves, the nourishment that allows us to breathe, to release what weighs us down.

The phrase, "apples don't fall far from the tree," reminds me of how I want my children to inherit these roots. But I want more for them than just to fall close to the tree; I want them to DIG. To know the roots beneath them, the stories that nourish them, and the struggles and triumphs that have shaped them. Too often, families keep parts of their stories hidden. We bury the painful parts, the shameful parts, believing it will protect the next generation. But what's buried grows unseen, sometimes in ways that twist and harm. When we bring our histories to the surface, we give them light, and light has a way of healing, of transforming.

Legacy is like tending a tree—nurturing its roots, honoring the strength of its trunk, and shaping its branches to grow with purpose. It's about recognizing when a part of the root needs pruning and when a cycle must be broken so that the whole tree can thrive. For my family, one of those deep, twisted roots has been fear. Fear that has clung to us, a root that seemed to choke off life's fullness. And I'm determined that this will not be my children's inheritance. I will prune that fear, tend to my roots, and nurture a legacy of grace and laughter.

There's a scene in *The Color Purple* that embodies this beautifully. It's a family dinner, and the tension at the table is thick—an unease everyone can feel as Celie, played by Whoopi

Goldberg, announces her decision to leave her husband, Mister, and move to Memphis with Shug Avery. The room holds its breath, bracing for Mister's explosive reaction. In the midst of this charged silence, Sofia, portrayed by Oprah Winfrey, breaks into a deep, soul-filled laugh that shatters the tension and transforms the atmosphere in an instant. Her laughter becomes healing—a release and a connection for everyone in the room. Laughter has the power to soften even the hardest moments, to reach across differences, and to find unity. That's what it does for roots, too—it brings healing, strength, and grace, giving us the room to breathe and grow.

We've all seen those wall decals and signs that say, *Live, Love, Laugh*. They seem so simple, maybe even overused, but I think there's real truth in those words. Living fully, loving deeply, and laughing freely—that's how roots grow strong. It's how we nourish what's beneath us, and it's how we pass down strength to those who come after us.

Because laughing at life's storms isn't about ignoring them—it's about facing them with resilience. It's knowing that roots, though unseen, are strong enough to withstand the winds and that storms cannot uproot a deeply grounded tree. When I laugh, I am connected to my ancestors, to my grandmother's twinkling eyes and my mother's gentle smile. In those moments of laughter, I am more alive, more grounded, more free. People who are afraid are not truly living, and I am here to live.

And so, I choose laughter. I choose resilience. I choose to DIG. I am my grandmother's child, my mother's daughter, and I am the roots that run through me.

 **Don't forget to laugh as you DIG:**

1. What family story has stuck with you? How has it shaped who you are today?

_____

_____

_____

2. Think of a time when humor or laughter shifted the mood in a difficult moment. How did it change things, and what did it teach you about resilience?

_____

_____

_____

3. If your roots could speak, what wisdom or lessons might they offer you?

_____

_____

_____

Continue to DIG

INTERLUDE

Rooted Values

A tree's strength doesn't come from what is seen—it comes from what lies beneath. Its roots stretch deep, unseen but essential, anchoring and nourishing everything above. But what grows from those roots? The fruit—the values that shape how we stand tall in the world.

This tree is full of possibilities, but its branches are waiting. What values have grown from your foundation?

Instructions:

1. Color the tree, letting yourself reflect on what has shaped you.

2. Write your values in the branches or leaves—words like faith, love, resilience, wisdom, kindness, grace, joy, courage.

3. If you wish, write what no longer serves you outside the tree, like fallen leaves that you are ready to let go of.

Every tree tells a story. What story does yours tell?

May you be open to develop in grace, standing tall and strong in the values that nourish you. **-DIG**

CHAPTER 9

Soft Soil for Tender Growth

"The soil is the great connector of lives,
the source and destination of all."
– Wendell Berry

As I reflect on my journey, I've come to understand that the softest soil—the gentlest and most tender parts of ourselves—is where the deepest growth occurs. It's in these vulnerable spaces that we can plant the seeds of our dreams, nurture them, and watch them grow into something both beautiful and resilient. Strength, as I once thought of it, was about being tough and unyielding. But the kind of strength that sustains, the kind I've learned to cultivate, is about allowing myself to be open, to soften, and to be willing to grow in ways I couldn't plan or predict.

Soft soil is not without its challenges. As soil needs to be tilled, watered, and cared for, so do we need to tend to our inner selves. Creating an environment where growth happens requires attention and care—allowing our roots to dig deep, find nourishment, and thrive. Perhaps it begins with tending to the unseen and deeply rooted, but maybe unevolved parts of who we are. I am mindful of a gardener who pulls up roots and fortifies the soil with nutrients, just as life's experiences and lessons, however hard and painful, can enrich and prepare us for greater growth if we allow them to.

There is something sacred about tending to this soil. For me, this often begins with stillness—a quieting of the noise within and around me. In these moments, I feel a deep connection to something greater than myself, a sense of divine presence guiding me through life's seasons. Whether it's through prayer, meditation, or simply taking time to pause, this connection replenishes me, helping me see the beauty in the process of growth, even when it feels uncertain or incomplete.

I've found that prayer, in its simplest form, is a grounding ritual that softens my soil. It's where I lay down my fears, my worries, and my need for control. It's a space where I surrender and allow grace to meet me right where I am. For some, this practice might look like quiet reflection, journaling, or a moment of gratitude, but for me, it's a dialogue with God that reminds me I'm never alone in this work of tending my garden.

The Gardener

The gardener in me is intentional, nurturing, and focused on growth. As a gardener, I tend to the soil of my life and the lives of those I love, planting seeds of grace, resilience, and connection. I prune away harmful patterns, just as a gardener trims dead branches to encourage new growth. Pruning is never easy—it can feel like loss before it feels like liberation—but it is always necessary.

The gardener also celebrates the beauty of each season. I've learned to honor the process, understanding that life doesn't rush its blooms. There's wisdom in knowing when to plant and water and when to wait. My tears, shed through seasons of pain, have softened the hardest soil in my life, allowing me to plant new dreams. I now see my experiences—both joyous and painful—as the nutrients that prepare the soil for my future growth.

The Groundskeeper

While the gardener focuses on nurturing specific plants, the groundskeeper takes a broader view, caring for the entire environment. The groundskeeper clears pathways, removes debris, and ensures that the larger system is stable and functional. In my life, this has meant addressing family dynamics, generational patterns, and relational systems that needed clearing and care.

I think of my brother's compost pile and the transformation it represents. Compost is made of things we discard, things that no longer serve their original purpose but which enrich the soil in ways we can't always see. In my own life, I've discarded outdated mindsets—perfectionism, fear of failure, and shame—and allowed them to become the rich compost that nourishes my growth. The groundskeeper in me ensures that I'm not just focused on what's blooming but also on clearing away what's preventing growth.

As a groundskeeper, I've had to create a safe and stable space for grace to take root. This work has been about maintaining the environment in which my family, my relationships, and my own spirit can flourish. It is not glamorous work, but it is essential. Clearing debris and stabilizing the foundation ensures that the garden—my life—can thrive. These roles—gardener and groundskeeper—are deeply intertwined. As a gardener, I tend to the delicate, intimate work of planting and nurturing. As a groundskeeper, I ensure the broader environment is stable and clear. Together, they allow me to cultivate a life that is rich with grace.

The Power of Surrender

Surrender has been one of the hardest but most necessary lessons in tending to my garden. I remember attending the final *Woman Thou Art Loosed* conference in Atlanta, GA. Priscilla Shirer spoke about letting go—allowing things to fall, fail, or even crumble so that something better could emerge. At the time, her words felt counterintuitive to everything I believed. But deep down, I knew the message was for me. It was time to stop clinging so tightly to the way I thought things should be and trust in something greater than myself.

When my marriage was falling apart, I had to surrender—not as a sign of defeat but as a way of softening the soil of my life. I let go of my need to control, fix, and fight. I turned to prayer, to stillness, and to grace, and in that surrender, I found renewal.

The gardener in me nurtured the soil with tears, love, and care, while the groundskeeper in me cleared the debris of resentment and hurt. Together, these roles allowed new life to emerge.

The 8 C's: Tools for Tending

I now turn to the 8 C's of self-leadership, a model created by Julia Sullivan and the IFS Institute, as my most effective strategies for self-care. These 8 C's have become my tools for tending to my inner garden and grounding me in who I am. Each "C" has a purpose:

- **Curiosity** reminds me to observe without judgment, seeing beauty even in my weeds.
- **Calm** helps me to let go of forcing outcomes, bringing peace where I used to feel pressure.
- **Confidence** reassures me that I have the ability to nurture growth, both within myself and in others.
- **Courage** lets me try new things, even if they're foreign or challenging, like planting unfamiliar flowers.

- **Creativity** invites me to dance to my own rhythm, making choices that feel right for me.

- **Connection** reminds me that I'm part of a larger community, a collective garden that we all tend together.

- **Compassion** allows my heart to shine fully, trusting that my feelings are both my strength and my guide.

- **Clarity** helps me hold to my vision as I let go of what no longer serves me.

Stepping Back to See the Garden

As I take a step back and survey my garden now, I see it as it is—a living, breathing tapestry of soft soil and resilient roots, tender blooms and fierce weeds, shaded corners, and open spaces. There is grace in each part, and strength lies not in its perfection but in its process. I am slowly learning to let the seasons guide me, rest when my soil needs replenishment, prune when I must, and nurture myself with curiosity, calm, and compassion. Each small victory, each gentle step forward, brings me closer to the tender growth that only soft soil can yield.

Don't forget your garden tools as you DIG:

WHAT A WAY TO CHALLENGE YOUR

READERS!!

1. How can you create the "soft soil" within yourself to nurture growth and healing?

_____

_____

_____

2. In what ways can you embrace the roles of gardener and groundskeeper in your life? Which role feels most natural, and which might require more intention?

_____

_____

_____

3. How can the 8 C's of self-leadership support you in clearing debris and tending to your personal growth?

_____

_____

_____

Continue to DIG

_____

_____

_____

_____

_____

_____

_____

_____

_____

_____

_____

_____

_____

_____

The Groundskeeper's Labor

By faith, the soil surrenders,

Opened by hands that know silence,

Seeds placed with quiet certainty—

Not seen, but always known.

With love, the roots are cradled,

Fed by the unseen,

Watered by whispers of grace,

Growing towards a light not yet visible.

Grace is the ground beneath us,

Soft in places, hard in others,

It holds us in the wait—

When nothing blooms, yet everything grows.

By hope, the earth is tended,

Each turn, each touch, a rhythm,

A slow, steady hum of life,

Unfolding, unseen, but felt.

Grace and patience guide the hands

Of those who till and tend.

For in this labor, quiet and constant,

We become—by faith, by love, by grace.

-DIG

CHAPTER 10

The Gift of Grace

*"You are breathing, you are living, you are
wrapped in endless, boundless grace."*
— Morgan Harper Nichols

Happy Birthday

Birthdays have always been complicated for me. Growing up as one of many children, birthdays weren't grand occasions. It wasn't that my birthday was forgotten—it just wasn't a big deal. Sharing a birthday month only added to the struggle. Over time, the expectations I carried turned into disappointments, and I told myself birthdays didn't really matter. But the deeper truth was, *If birthdays didn't matter, then I didn't matter.*

That belief became an undercurrent in my life, shaping how I approached celebrations—not just for myself, but for others. I started downplaying my own milestones, convincing myself they weren't important. I became the planner in my family— the one who celebrated everyone else. Birthdays, baby showers, milestones, holidays, and even a wedding, I poured my heart into making these moments special for others. But when it came to me, I felt invisible. No one made the same effort, and the ache of that truth was too much to face.

Over time, that ache turned into avoidance. The more I tried to suppress the hurt, the less I felt capable of planning anything at all. My inability to face those feelings paralyzed me. When my mom retired after 30 years of government service, she wanted to celebrate that incredible milestone. I wanted to plan something for her, too—something meaningful that would honor her years of dedication. But as I sat with the weight of trying to make it happen, I became overwhelmed. The thought of planning brought back all the fear and anxiety of falling short. I felt like I didn't have the support I needed, and I could already hear the echo of her disappointment if it didn't turn out the way I envisioned. That fear became so heavy that I let the plans stay in my head, and I never found the strength to move forward.

This same anxiety and fear followed me into my role as a mother. My son and daughter experienced many home birthday celebrations because I couldn't bear the pressure of a party. I told myself I hated birthday parties and even bad-mouthed parents who went all out for their children's celebrations, but deep down, I wasn't being honest—with myself or with my children. Beneath the surface, it wasn't about disliking parties.

It was about the hurt I carried and the fear of not being enough. My children noticed my tension around birthdays and saw how I avoided the idea of a party, offering everything else under the sun as a substitute. The hurt I hadn't addressed became a barrier not just for me but for them.

Grace in the Support of Others

Everything began to shift when I allowed myself to open. A few years ago, I shared my struggles with a group of women I had grown close to. I told them about my complicated relationship with birthdays, how I had

"...grace is full of give and take."

convinced myself they didn't matter, and how hard it was to plan anything because of the weight of my own expectations. Their response was immediate and full of grace: "Oh no, we're celebrating *your* birthday."

And they did. That birthday became a turning point. For the first time in a long time, I felt loved, valued, and seen. It wasn't the size of the celebration that mattered—it was the simple act of being embraced by others who truly cared. It showed me that I didn't need to carry the burden alone and that I could be celebrated in ways that felt true to who I was.

This experience helped me see my family in a new light. As I reflected on my journey, I realized that my family had always supported me, even if it didn't look the way I expected. When I shared my plan to finish my book for my 40th birthday, their response revealed the depth of their care. It wasn't in grand gestures or elaborate displays but in their intrigue and thoughtful questions and the glint in their eyes. It was in the way they listened, made plans to come to town, and asked how they could help.

In their own quiet way, they reminded me that grace is full of give and take. Sometimes, it shows up as a loud celebration; other times, it's in the subtle ways people lean in, supporting and reminding us that we are seen, valued, and loved. Grace isn't always loud or obvious; sometimes, it's in the quiet presence of people who simply stand with us.

Grace is Simple

As I've navigated these experiences, I've come to understand that grace itself is simple. I've always been a simple kind of girl, finding joy in the little things: a warm mug of tea in the morning, sunlight filtering through the curtains, or laughter shared over a meal. And yes, finishing this book is a big deal, but at its core, it is grace personified.

Grace doesn't demand perfection. It isn't flashy or adorned with frills. It's something we allow ourselves to experience—a gift that doesn't require us to accomplish or perform. It doesn't boastfully announce its arrival. Grace isn't the grand gift wrapped in a bow under a Christmas tree. No, grace is the breeze that cools you on a hot day. It's the way the first sip of coffee or tea (for me, thank you) soothes your soul or the way a stranger's smile can lift your spirits.

Grace is in the rain that waters the earth after a dry spell, the hug that melts away a long day's tension, and the laughter that bursts forth unexpectedly during a tough time. It's the handwritten note from a friend, the way your favorite song plays just when you need it, or the stillness of a quiet morning where nothing is pressing except the peace you feel in your heart.

The Gift of Grace

When I slowed down to ask myself what I truly wanted for my 40th birthday, grace showed up with its quiet clarity: *Finish your book*. It was a gift I didn't know I needed—a way to honor my journey, reflect on my growth, and give back to others. In that moment, I remembered a truth that has carried me through life's heaviest seasons: *"My grace is sufficient for you, for my power is made perfect in weakness."* (2 Corinthians 12:9 NIV). These words have always felt like a balm to my soul, a reminder that grace isn't about what I bring to the table—it's about what God has already provided. Sufficiency doesn't mean ease or abundance; it means trust. It means knowing that I don't have to have all the answers or carry every burden because grace fills the gaps where I cannot.

> *"Grace doesn't demand performance or striving; it simply invites me to let go and receive what is already present"*

This sufficiency shows up in the quietest ways, in the most unexpected moments. It's in the stillness of a morning walk, in the laughter of my children, in the peace that comes when I finally allow myself to rest. Grace doesn't demand performance or striving; it simply invites me to let go and receive what is already present in and around me. Grace showed up as a gentle reminder that I didn't need to meet anyone else's expectations. I didn't need to make my birthday a grand event or perform for the approval of others. Grace whispered, *You are enough. Your life, your story, your journey—they are already worthy of celebration.*

This book is my gift of grace to myself and to the world. It is a reflection of all I've learned about digging deep, embracing imperfection, and trusting the process. Each page is a testament to the ways grace has carried me—through storms, transitions, and moments of doubt—and the ways it continues to sustain me.

The Simplicity of Grace

Life is much like tending a garden. There are seasons of planting and seasons of waiting. There are weeds that challenge us, rain that nourishes us, and unexpected blossoms that remind us of the beauty of growth.

Grace is the constant gardener, showing up in those quiet moments to nourish, heal, and encourage us to keep growing. It's the sunlight breaking through on a cloudy day, the unexpected kindness of a friend, or the peace that washes over you in the stillness of prayer.

Grace, like the changing seasons, comes in waves. There's a time for blooming, a time for resting, a time for shedding, and a time for growth. It's not always loud or obvious, but it is always present, patiently waiting for us to notice its gentle rhythm.

Grace is not about perfection or grandeur—it's about presence. It's a gentle reminder that even in our imperfections, we are worthy of love, joy, and connection.

 ## Reflection Questions

1. What if you gave yourself permission to see grace in your own life?

   _____

   _____

   _____

2. What is one gift you can give yourself that reflects who you truly are?

   _____

   _____

   _____

3. In what ways can you recognize and embrace the support of those around you?

   _____

   _____

   _____

4. How might your life look if you celebrated you and others more—not because you or they earned it, but because you and they are already worthy?

_____

_____

_____

Continue to DIG

_____

_____

_____

_____

_____

_____

_____

_____

_____

_____

_____

_____

_____

_____

_____

The Great Grace Chase

Imagine yourself running through a field, legs pumping, heart racing. You're chasing something elusive, something just out of reach. It's grace.

But here's the twist—grace isn't running away. It's sitting there, calm and serene, probably sipping tea, wondering why you're making such a fuss.

Why chase what's already yours? Grace isn't a prize to be won; it's as free as the air you're breathing, as constant as the ground beneath your feet. It's right there, waiting for you to stop running, to notice it's been there all along.

So the next time you find yourself in pursuit of grace, pause. Look around. Grace is already there, smiling at you, waiting for you to see it.

You're welcome.

-DIG

CHAPTER 11

The Next Chapter in Grace

"What lies behind us and what lies before us are tiny matters compared to what lies within us."
– Ralph Waldo Emerson

It's funny how, when you begin to focus on something, it starts to show up everywhere. Recently, grace has been all around me—woven into conversations, shimmering in quiet moments, present in the way I now experience and witness life. My "grace sense" feels heightened, as if I've tuned into a frequency that has always been there, waiting for me to listen. Grace has become my companion and a gentle reminder, offering me an extra breath before I respond or react, inviting me to live slower, softer. Grace is woven into the very fabric of humanity. Across cultures, traditions, and beliefs, the concept of grace echoes a universal truth: life isn't always fair, and yet, grace steps in to fill the gaps. Whether we call it kindness, mercy, or divine favor, grace reminds us that we don't have to earn love or worthiness—it is simply given.

In the Bible, grace is mentioned over 170 times (source: Bible Gateway), underscoring its centrality in God's relationship with humanity. While the Christian faith points to Jesus as the ultimate expression of grace, the idea of grace extends beyond any single belief system. It's what moves us to forgive when it feels impossible, to show compassion to the hurting, and to find strength in our brokenness.

Grace is the quiet force that reminds us of our shared humanity. It acknowledges that life, with all its beauty and pain, requires something greater than ourselves to sustain us. For me, grace points to Jesus—a Savior who didn't just preach love but lived

"Grace is the quiet force reminds us of our shared humanity."

it, offering grace to the overlooked, the weary, and the brokenhearted. And yet, even for those who don't share this faith, grace remains a lifeline. It meets us where we are and asks nothing in return.

Worth It Work of Grace

Developing in grace—or engaging in DIG—is messy work, much like digging into the soil. It requires effort, patience, and a willingness to get your hands dirty. But, as I like to call it, it's *worth it work*. It's the kind of effort that transforms, even as it challenges, uncovering the roots of who we are and making space for new growth. *Candice, oh Candice, how does your garden grow?* In grace. Grace that allows for mistakes, growth, and learning. Grace shows me that even the messiest gardens can bloom beautifully.

Grace is teaching me that I don't have to be everywhere and do everything all the time. I no longer feel the need to attend every event or say yes to every invitation. Grace tells me, *It's okay to rest. Your presence isn't required at every gathering.* And so, I trust that others will understand, that they will have grace for me, just as I have learned to understand and hold space for them. And for those who don't or won't? Well, there's grace for them too.

This newfound trust, this easing of expectations, feels like uncharted territory for me. Throughout my life, I've often lived in extremes. I went from being a timid, bullied child to someone who, as my daughter would put it after a playground scuffle, responded with, "We was fighting." My reaction was my armor—my way of shielding myself from vulnerability and pain. Toughness became my default, a badge I wore to protect the tender places within me.

But as I've grown, grace has become a transformative force, softening the edges of that armor. I've come to understand that true strength isn't found in being loud or defensive. It doesn't lie in the clenched fists or the unyielding walls we build around our hearts. Grace has taught me that resilience is quieter and softer. It's in the ability to let go, to release the weight of things that no longer serve us, and to trust in a deeper flow—a flow that carries us forward, even when we're unsure of where it leads.

Now, a tear in my eye doesn't mean a battle. Tears, once symbols of resistance and conflict, have become moments of release, grace-filled and healing. They're reminders of the strength found in vulnerability and the beauty of allowing emotions to flow freely, untethered by the need to prove or protect. I've learned that some things are simply worth letting go.

Planting Seeds, Nurturing Dreams

As I reflect on the journey that brought me here, especially on the brink of a new decade, I feel a profound shift within me. Grace feels good on me. Turning 40 feels like stepping into a new way of living—one that is guided by ease, faith, and a focus on nurturing my strengths rather than fixing my flaws. Grace looks good on me. This, I believe, is the essence of aging gracefully: not only in appearance but through the quiet, inward work that shapes how we carry ourselves. It's growing softer, showing compassion, and trusting the natural flow of life.

One of the most powerful lessons I learned came during a life group meeting when our facilitator shared, *"You can work on your weaknesses, but there's greater power in building on your strengths."* This was a revelation. For so long, I had been focused on "fixing" myself, smoothing out every rough edge, strengthening every flaw. That approach pushed me to grow but also left me weary—my spirit drained by the weight of constant striving. Now, I am choosing to lean into what comes naturally, the gifts that bring me joy, the places where I feel most at ease.

The past decade has been a time of deep digging—digging into my experiences, unearthing traumas, and reconnecting with my roots. I've spent years tending the soil, planting seeds, and nurturing the garden of my life. Grace has shown me that growth isn't only about pushing through hard ground; it's also about finding space to rest and rejuvenate. Just as a garden needs time to flourish, so do our dreams and aspirations. In this season, I'm learning to allow things to grow at their own pace without rushing or forcing.

Aging gracefully, I'm discovering, isn't something that happens on the surface. It's the result of the inner work—the compassion we cultivate, the judgments we release, and the grace we extend to ourselves. I'm no longer carrying the weight of self-expectation, of feeling I must meet every challenge alone. I'm learning that strength lies in asking for help, trusting others to share the load, and balancing my life with a gentleness I hadn't known before.

Like the roots of a tree, my family, faith, and friendships keep me grounded through every season. These connections nourish me, providing strength even as I change and grow. I've come to appreciate the importance of surrounding myself with people who uplift me, just as a tree's roots are strengthened by those around it. This next chapter is not just about my growth; it's about contributing to the growth of others. Whether through my professional endeavors, life groups, mentoring, leading children's church, or simply being present for my loved ones, I am committed to cultivating a garden that nourishes not just me but everyone I'm connected to.

One of the most exciting aspects of this chapter is the freedom it brings—the freedom to explore, to create, and to express myself without the rigid

"...growth isn't always beautiful, but it is divine."

constraints that once held me back. I am entering this season with an open heart, ready to embrace new experiences, connections, and ways of sharing my gifts. It's a season of reaping what I've sown but also of planting new seeds for the future, nurturing dreams yet to come.

As I look back on the road I've traveled, I'm filled with gratitude for every trial, every triumph, every tear. They have all led me here to a place of balance, peace, and grace. And so, as I step forward, I am ready to dig deeper into the soil of grace, to nurture the seeds of my dreams, and to witness them bloom in their time.

Grace is the soil from which we grow, nurturing our roots even when the ground feels hard. It is the quiet force that supports our growth, often unseen but always present. Grace has been my guide, my teacher, my constant. It has taught me to soften, to trust, and to embrace each season with openness. And it will carry me forward into this next chapter with strength, resilience, and a heart ready for the beauty still to come.

Continue to DIG

_____

_____

_____

_____

_____

_____

_____

_____

_____

_____

_____

_____

_____

_____

Grace War Cry

There was a shout before victory

I felt my help coming

I paused for the cause

My mind ceased running

Tic tock, it did stop

Gasp turned deep

Breath released

Fearlessly I walked

Beyond original belief

Time tells the strong do last

Not a product of

Yet, I'll never forget my past

Pressure turned gold

Releasing unbridled soul

Cry out

More roar than bark

More feast than famine

Let it rain; let it pour

A thirsty soul no more

Adorned with grace

I took my place

V for victory

Before victory, God is always near.

I will trust in Him; whom shall I fear?

His Son did the bid for my sin.

Victory is mine by the name of Grace.

Now watch as I rise from the depths of the soil,

Connected by roots, stretching towards light.

My war cry echoes strong and clear,

With Grace as my shield, I have no fear.

Together, we're rooted by Grace's decree—

Live free and **DIG**.

Tis the Season for Grace

*To everything, there is a season, and a time
to every purpose under heaven.*
(Ecclesiastes 3:1, New International Version)

There is a mystery to the seasons, a grace woven into each one that holds us, molds us, and makes us who we are. Each season bears a gift—though often hidden—that helps us dig deeper, stretching us beyond what we can see.

As I sit here, reflecting on the seasons I have lived, I feel the weight of them—not as a burden, but as a tapestry woven with moments of struggle and joy, loss and discovery. Each one has shaped me, leaving its imprint, teaching me something about who I am and who I am becoming.

I think back to my younger self, a girl with trembling hands and an anxious heart, standing in my grandmother's church, feeling the press of eyes and expectations. In that small, pivotal moment, I first glimpsed the battle within me—the desire to be seen and the fear of standing in the light. Even as a child, grace was there, nudging me along, whispering, *You are worthy. You are enough*.

That was only the beginning. Over time, each season has brought its own challenges and joys, each one revealing more of who I am and inviting me to dig deeper into grace.

When we're young, life feels like an endless field ripe for planting. We cannot yet see what lies beneath the soil or know what the years will bring. But I planted my seeds with faith, with a heart that knew God would tend to them. Growing up as the eldest girl of five in a military family, I learned early the weight of responsibility, a weight I carried almost too eagerly—one that, over time, became both **a burden and a badge of honor.** Yet, as the years passed, I saw those seeds begin to grow — slowly, tended by God's appointed groundskeeper—into a deep-rooted understanding of who I am and whose I am. I began to realize that my purpose was never to seek, strive, push, or stress.

Now, I stand in my garden—DIGging not just to break the ground, but to tend what's growing, to trust what's unseen, and to rest in the grace that sustains it all. Still, there are moments that remain etched in me—formative seasons that shaped my faith, my fears, and my understanding of grace. I remember the season as a teen when I first felt the true joy of being held by something greater, the joy of salvation that became a quiet fire within me, a sanctuary I could return to no matter what storms came my way. Just as a tree's growth begins underground, where no one can see, so too did my growth in grace begin there, unseen yet deeply rooted.

Then there were the seasons of pruning when I learned that not everything we cling to is meant to stay. Pruning taught me the sacred art of letting go. In love and in loss, grace taught me to release what was no longer serving me, even when it felt painful. My marriage, a sacred and profound journey, bore both joy and betrayal. There were moments when I thought we would not make it, times when I considered walking away. Yet grace showed up, steady and sure, guiding us back to each other, asking me to let go of the old wounds, the competition, the pride that kept us apart. Grace taught me to forgive not only him but myself—to surrender, to let go, and to see love in its truest form like a tree shedding its leaves to make way for new growth.

Winter brings its own kind of beauty, a stillness that can be mistaken for silence. In the waiting, life stirs beneath the ice, preparing for what is to come. My years as a hospice worker were like that—quiet, sacred times of witnessing the fragility of life and the rawness of grief. Grace anchored me, teaching me the depth of stillness, how to sit in silence, wait, and trust that even in the hardest seasons, there is purpose.

I remember watching the lake near my home, its surface still and cold, but knowing that beneath lay unseen life. That winter season mirrored my inner life, a time when grace taught me to be patient with myself, to allow the quiet to reveal what needed to be healed. My children, in their resilience, reflected this grace back to me, offering new mercies each day, reminding me that grace waits for us until we are ready to grow.

And then there are seasons when everything blooms, when all that was hidden beneath the soil springs forth, and you see the fruits of your labor, of faith, and of resilience. I think of my work as a counselor, as a mother, as a woman striving to live in grace. Each role has been shaped by seeds sown in faith and watered by resilience. My son's and daughter's battles reflect so much of me and require me to dig deeper to nurture a love that grows over time through trial and error, forgiveness, and the breaking of the soil. Their capacity for grace, their willingness to give new mercies every day, has shown me what grace truly is—an invitation to grow, to bloom, to become.

These seasons of blooming have been the richest of my life, not because they were easy but because they were holy. Grace met me in the trenches of parenting, in the sacred silence of hospice rooms, in the fiery trials of marriage, and in the secret garden of my silent turmoil. It whispered, *Keep going; I'm here.* Grace taught me that growth isn't always beautiful, but it is always divine.

Each season has left its mark on me, etching its lessons into my spirit. I am who I am because of these seasons—not in spite of them, but because of them. I had to live, go through, grow through each stage, and develop in grace. To become the woman sitting here now, penning these words, knowing that each story, each heartache, each joy was woven with a purpose that stretches beyond me.

And so, I offer this book as a testament to grace. My hope is that it reflects the seasons you've walked through, offers companionship in the ones still unfolding, and reminds you that every stage—whether it feels like winter's stillness or summer's abundance—is shaping who you are becoming. Trust the season you are in. Let grace do its work.

And remember:

- There is a time for **digging** and a time for **planting**.
- A time for **pruning** and a time for **weeping**.
- A time for **waiting** and a time for **the harvest**.
- And when the harvest comes, **may you savor its sweetness. May you enjoy the fruits of your labor.**

And may you always, always **DIG.**

DIG Affirmations

Cultivating Grace Through Affirmations- Be Still and Know that you are... Stillness is not for the Affirmations, which are more than just words; they are seeds planted in the fertile soil of your heart and mind. In moments of doubt, growth, or transition, these affirmations act as reminders to anchor yourself in grace—a place of softness and strength, vulnerability and courage, progress and patience. They call you to DIG: to develop in grace, to delve into the depths of who you are, and to rise rooted in your truth.

Each affirmation invites you to pause, breathe, and reflect. They are not demands for perfection but gentle nudges to embrace the journey of becoming. Whether you're facing life's storms, tending to the soil of your soul or stretching toward the light, these affirmations remind you that grace is always present—

flowing in the stillness, holding you steady, and whispering that you are enough.

Let these affirmations guide you as you DIG deep to grow, honoring the seasons of your life and the resilience that comes from being deeply rooted in grace.

I am the rhythm of the earth, steady and sure.

I am the echo of prayers whispered long before my time.

I am light finding its way through cracks of darkness.

I am a vessel of stillness and strength.

I am the stillness that steadies the storm.

I am a voice of encouragement; I speak life to others.

I am a bearer of forgiveness.

I am a source of hope.

I am a gardener of beauty.

I am calm, centered, and clear.

I am becoming who I am.

I can, and I will develop in grace.

I am rooted in love, growing in grace.

I am the quiet force that moves mountains.

I am the keeper of peace, even in chaos.

I am the breath of renewal, the pause that heals.

I am the flame that warms, not burns.

I am a reflection of the divine, whole, and radiant.

I am the bridge between what was and what can be.

I am a sanctuary of grace and compassion.

I am the ripple that becomes the wave.

I am the harmony of strength and softness.

I am a witness to life's beauty, even in the hard places.

I am the bloom that follows the rain.

I am the courage to rise and the wisdom to rest.

I am a thread in the tapestry of grace woven with purpose.

I am a reminder that light always finds a way.

APPENDIX B

Go Forth and DIG

As you close this chapter, take with you the lessons of grace as a guide to continue developing in grace—deepening your roots, nurturing your growth, and embracing the journey ahead.

1. **D – Develop:**

   - Reflect on how grace has shaped your life up to this point. Where can you allow more room for grace to guide your development? Consider the areas where you can let go, trust, and allow grace to soften and strengthen you.

2. **I – In (Inward):**

   - Turn inward to recognize your gifts, strengths, and natural inclinations. How can you honor what already comes naturally to you, focusing on nurturing what brings you joy and fulfillment? Embrace the grace in valuing your authentic self.

3. **G – Grace (Grow):**

- Envision the growth you hope to cultivate in this new season. How will you carry grace into this chapter of your life? Allow yourself to grow with ease, trusting that grace will support and guide you as you take each step forward.

Go forth and DIG—Develop in Grace. Trust that grace is always present, nourishing and grounding you through every season. As you continue your journey, remember to develop in grace, to embrace both the strength and softness it offers, and to walk forward rooted, resilient, and ready for what's to come.

Cited References

Adele, D. (2009). The Yamas & Niyamas: Exploring Yoga's Ethical Practice. On-Word Bound Books.

Bible Gateway. "Grace." Accessed November 2025. www.biblegateway.com.

Holy Bible, New International Version. (2011). Biblica, Inc. https://www.biblica.com/niv/.

Liebscher, B. (2016). Rooted: The Hidden Places Where God Develops You. Waterbrook.

Phillips, A. (2022). The garden within: Where the war with your emotions ends and your most powerful life begins. HarperCollins Leadership.

Schwartz, R. C. (1995). Internal Family Systems Therapy. Guilford Press.

Spielberg, S. (Director). (1985). The Color Purple [Film]. Warner Bros.

Wohlleben, P. (2016). The hidden life of trees: What they feel, how they communicate –

Discoveries from a secret world (J. Billinghurst, Trans.). Greystone Books.

Van der Kolk, B. A. (2014). The body keeps the score: Brain, mind, and body in the healing of trauma. Viking.

Author Biography

Candice Evans is a mom, wife, sister, daughter, friend—and all things human. She holds a Bachelor's in Psychology from Saint Louis University and a Master of Science in Social Work from the University of Louisville. As a Licensed Clinical Social Worker, Candice has supported countless individuals through life's transitions, creating space for thousands of stories filled with resilience, vulnerability, and grace. As founder of Develop in Grace, Candice helps individuals, families, groups, leaders, and organizations DIG through counseling, coaching, consultation, and creative expression. With a unique approach that blends humor with heartfelt insight and critical thinking, Candice draws on her diverse lived experiences, professional expertise and deep curiosity about the human experience and condition to inspire others to navigate life's challenges with resilience and purpose.

Her work is both transformative and relative, helping people to DIG deep to cultivate growth and navigate the ever-changing garden of life.

A proud "military brat" with travel tales from across the globe, Candice's early years sparked her love for diverse stories. An introverted processor and lifelong dreamer, she's often been told, "You need to write a book!" or "That should be a movie!" Her first published work, **DIG: Develop in Grace**, is the culmination of her experiences, passions, and commitment to helping others grow in grace. The book reflects her belief that even messy work—like digging into life's challenges—can lead to transformation and growth.

Through her work and life, Candice has witnessed how deeply people can be burdened by their past, their imperfections, and circumstances both within and beyond their control. She offers a simple but profound call: more kindness, more compassion, more love, more laughter, more space—and above all, more grace. She credits grace with saving her when guilt, shame, anger, anxiety, depression and fear felt overwhelming, teaching her to stop fighting and start DIGging. Her hope is that each reader will feel empowered to heal, grow, connect, and shine when they begin to DIG. Candice's energy is a vibe, and she knows she's her best self when she's floating through life like a butterfly—light, free, and fully herself. And "Hey, Oprah! " That's Candice's way of saying hello to the icon she's always dreamed of meeting. If you know, you know.

When she's not writing, Candice loves to dance—even to a beat only she can hear—and stays active through group fitness, connecting with girlfriends, and exploring new places with her family. She is deeply involved in her church and community, finding joy in helping others and healing. Most days, you'll find her balancing family life, her professional calling, and her endless creativity and curiosity.

For those who cross her path, it's clear that Candice is always dreaming up something meaningful and new. DIG is the first published book in Candice's growing body of work—stay tuned for the stories, wisdom, and movement yet to come!

Stay connected to Candice and DIG community:

- Sign up for mailing list at www.developingrace.com Be the first to know about new projects, exclusive goodies and content, and special DIG opportunities and merch.

- Follow on social media @developingrace. Join the conversation and be part of the journey.

- Let's Collaborate! Direct inquiries for an interview, featured conversation or collaborative oportunity to info@developingrace.com.

- Follow You & Your Journey: use #DIG and share your story to myDIGstory@developingrace.com.

- Leave a review on Amazon, Goodreads or wherever you purchased DIG. Your words and story about the impact of DIG will help others discover the power of grace.

Thank you!

www.ingramcontent.com/pod-product-compliance
Lightning Source LLC
Chambersburg PA
CBHW021139130626
46554CB00005B/1572